MINI ENCYCLOPEDIA OF
RABBIT
BREEDS & CARE

MINI ENCYCLOPEDIA OF
RABBIT
BREEDS & CARE

A guide to caring for your rabbit

Geoff Russell

INTERPET
PUBLISHING

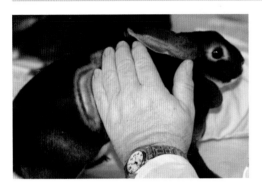

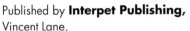

Published by **Interpet Publishing,**
Vincent Lane,
Dorking,
Surrey RH4 3YX
England

© 2008 Interpet Publishing Ltd.
All rights reserved
This reprint 2010
ISBN 9781842862056

Editor: **Candida Buckley**
Designer: **Sue Rose**
Photography: **Neil Robertson**

Production Management: **Colin Gower Enterprises Ltd.**
Pre-press: **AGP Repro Hong Kong Ltd.**
Print Production: **1010 Printing International Ltd**

This book sets out to:
provide a complete guide to rabbit breeds and how to maintain a rabbit in good health and happiness for the span of its life. If followed, the programme and techniques contained in this book will reap results. Health and Safety issues pointed out by the author should be heeded, particularly washing after contact with your pet. It is important too, to realise that some rabbits are not suitable for children's pets and the breed section gives advice on this. In all cases of illness it is advisable to seek the advice of a qualified Veterinarian.

The Author

Geoff Russell is a retired Education Officer who for many years was Britain's top breeder and exhibitor of the most ancient exhibition breed, the English Lop. Geoff has also been a British Rabbit Council District Advisor and Judge.

Geoff is well known throughout the rabbit fancy in many parts of the world for the numerous magazine articles he has written on rabbit related topics. He has published three books about rabbits, *A Fancier's Guide to the Lop Rabbit*, *Showing Rabbits* and *The English Lop* (all of which are available from the *Fur and Feather* book shop). He is probably best known for his long-running monthly column in *Fur and Feather* which was entitled 'Notes from the Shed'.

Geoff has recently retired from the exhibition rabbit world and lives with his wife, Lynn, in Cambridgeshire.

Contents

PART ONE

Your Rabbit: Getting Started

1 • *A Short History*

The Domestication of the Rabbit

Early Domestication

The rabbit is known by the Latin name, *cuniculus* (burrower), a name that Linnaeus conferred on it when he published his classifications of flora and fauna in the mid eighteenth century. Varro (116 – 27 BC), the Governor of Spain, wrote his treatise on farming entitled *De Re Rustica*, which included a description of the rabbit. He wrote: *'Everyone knows, too, that if you put in but a few hares of both sexes, the warren will swarm with them in a short time, so prolific is the quadruped …often when a litter has not long been born, they are found to have others inside them'* and again later *'There is also the recent fashion, now general, of fattening them – by taking them from the warren, shutting them up in cages, and fattening them in confinement'.* Almost certainly Varro is in fact talking about rabbits rather than hares, as hares are unlikely to 'swarm in a short time' or to breed in a warren. And as we shall see later it is this start of selective breeding, domestication and fattening in an enclosed environment that was many centuries later to produce all the various breeds that we see today.

In the 'Natural History' written by Pliny the Elder (c. 23-79 AD), he tells us how from one pair of escaped rabbits in the Balearic Islands, that the islands became so infested with wild rabbits which destroyed the inhabitants crops and even undermined their houses with their burrows so that the people had to apply to Emperor Augustus of Rome for assistance from his troops to prevent further damage. Pliny records that the troops were sent along with ferrets to destroy the rabbits.

It is believed that the rabbit actually originated in Spain or at least in the Iberian Peninsula. But it was the Romans who discovered that rabbits kept in cages could successfully be bred from so that the rabbit became a portable meat (and fur) source for their armies, thus ensuring its distribution throughout the Roman Empire. The cage required to house a rabbit is relatively small, making it ideal for transportation on the ship. One can easily imagine multiple cages of rabbits being kept on the Roman ships to supply the crews and the armies they were transporting. The early coloniser's journeys were often very lengthy and the rabbit's short gestation period (30–32 days) would mean the travellers could actually replenish their supplies during the voyage. If this theory is accepted then it is easy to see how the Romans spread rabbits throughout their dominions. They were equally responsible for the spread of pheasant, quail and the edible door mouse – all things they liked to eat. If the Romans did bring rabbits into England then they did not survive probably because of the range of carnivorous predators that roamed the country at that time.

Domestication

The domestication of the wild rabbit almost certainly started in Roman times with the

Thetford Warren Lodge

In the middle of many old warrens, there stood a single, small building, called the Warren lodge. The most famous lodges were found in the Brecklands of Norfolk, and some date back to the fifteenth century. The Thetford Lodge had walls over three feet thick made of local flint. The roof was thatched and there was a staircase from the ground floor to the second storey. The ground floor would have been very gloomy because there was only a single door and window. There were racks for drying rabbit skins, and for storing nets and big lanterns for night work. The lodge, standing on the highest part of the warren, was exposed to winds from all directions. The

keeper (or Warrener) often went to the top of his 'lookout' to make sure that his rabbits were in no danger.

caging of rabbits for fattening, breeding or transportation over land or sea. Two opposing theories are put forward as to the evolutionary effects of the caging of rabbits:

➤ If the caged animals are killed for food and fur then it is these tamer, animals that will continually be eliminated, leaving the wild rabbits to proliferate. Thus caging does not enhance domestication.

➤ If, as may well have been likely, the caged (and tamer) does are left alive to have more litters then it is in fact the caged (or tamer)

animals that are continually being bred from thus furthering the domestication of the species. Therefore caging enhances the development of the domesticated rabbit.

Whichever of these theories you choose to go with, the caging of rabbits has to be considered within the overall picture; rabbits have been managed by man, and thrived, in a variety of situations for at least the last two millennium: Three main systems have been used to rear rabbits for food and their fur:

• Rabbits Warrens

11

A Warrener

Warrens or Coningrys were established primarily to protect wild rabbits from carnivorous predators and in doing so protecting a valuable meat and fur source, of course the containment of the rabbits also protected the crops from their destructiveness. Warrens were first noted in England during the Norman period when the entourage of any self respecting Norman Baron would have a Warrener and his ferrets. It was Giraldus, the 12th century Welsh historian, who stated that each feudal lord had his private army, his fishponds and his rabbit warren. At about the

A warrener or rabbit keeper

same time and for much the same reasons rabbit warrens were being established in France.

- Rabbit Gardens or Courts
- Rabbit Islands

Rabbit Warrens were fenced or walled

areas that allow the rabbits to burrow into the enclosed mounds and therefore live as 'wild rabbits'. Some warrens spread over many acres, in fact large tracts of Norfolk, England were said to be more profitable under rabbits than cultivation.

Warrens can be sub divided into those from which the rabbits are taken for food and fur and those that are used to raise rabbits that are then deliberately released into the wild to be hunted for sport. The Warrens that kept rabbits for food and fur were a substantial source of income to their owners for many generations. The Warrens on the large estates of England

that bred rabbits to be released for rough game shooting continued right up till just after the Second World War.

The disease myxomatosis was to have a devastating effect on the population of wild rabbits in Britain during the 1950's and although the wild rabbit population has by now all but recovered, many warrens never did.

Rabbit Court or Garden The Rabbit

Court was a much smaller affair than the Rabbit Warren; the enclosed rabbits were allowed to run free within an enclosed area whilst a degree of management was applied to maximise and control the production of stock.

We know from historical records that Rabbit Courts, probably very similar in many ways to

From **The Rabbit Book for the Many**
(The Journal of Horticulture and Poultry Chronicle 1867).

I shall take note of something extraordinary relating to a warren, as it was contriv'd and practis'd by the late Lady Belassis at Kensington; her ladyship, among many other curiosities which were cultivated in her gardens, and volaries, disposed one part for the breeding and feeding of Rabbets, in such a manner, as that, by a constant supply of nourishing food, she might draw at any time of the year a sufficient quantity to oblige her friends, and serve her table; but to prevent unsavoury taste which generally attends the flesh of tame Rabbets, consulted as much as possible the nature of the wild sort, how much the open air was beneficial to them, for this end she wall'd in a large square place, and paved it at the bottom, but in some parts had large heaps of earth, ram'd hard, and turf'd, for them to burrow in; but this, which was her first attempt, fail'd, by frequently falling in upon the Rabbets: This however gave her no discouragement; she had a terrass built with arches, and fill'd with earth, leaving proper places for the Rabbets to go in and out; but still there were many inconveniences, as the falling in of the earth, and males destroying the young ones besides the difficulty of taking them when they are wanted; but at length concluded to build distinct cells for every female, so order'd that they might hide themselves at pleasure, or take the liberty of the enclos'd ground when they thought fit: these cells were cover'd with boards, lying penthouse-wise, made to open at discretion, for the better catching the Rabbets, and to prevent the destroying of does that had young ones: Over the entrance of every cell was a trap – door; either for keeping them in or out: at the south end was a covered place where a couple of buck Rabbets were chain'd for service of the does, and, according to the warreners rule, were enough for twenty – five couples of females: In this place was their food, which was chiefly the refuse of the garden, with some bran and oats, and large blocks of chaulk stone, which they frequently eat to prevent the rot. The pavement or floor was lay'd slopewise for better carrying off the water, and conveniency of cleaning, which was done very often, and contributed greatly to the good thriving of the Rabbets.'

the one described above, had been employed in monasteries since before the fifth century and that it was in these courts that selection began to take place as different colours and mutations occurred. If we want to select a point in history when the domestication of the wild rabbit started we would almost certainly have to select The Papal Edict issued by Pope Gregory the Great in 600AD.

Gregory, the first monk ever to be chosen as Pope, decreed that rabbits (or more correctly the unborn young or pre-firred young) were not

Church pew showing hare.

to be classed as a meat and could therefore be eaten by the monks during Lent. This allowed the Monks to adopt the Roman habit of eating unborn or new born rabbits, which were called Laurices. The rabbit was an ideal source of protein, and the fur provided warm clothing for the Monks in their closed societies. Both these desirable features doubtless being selectively bred into the types of rabbit the monks kept. Perhaps one of the other features to be selectively bred was tameness; Darwin (1867) states that 'Wild rabbits, if taken young, can be domesticated, though the process is generally troublesome' and one would tend to feel that those rabbits bred and raised in an enclosed court would over numerous successive generations come to naturally accept man's presence even if it was only when the human came to feed them. Similarly, one can see that if rabbits kept within a courtyard were able to run away from man, even if not very far away, they would not become domesticated to any extent.

Rabbit Islands

Before leaving the early warrens and rabbit courts we must briefly mention the Rabbit Island, for this was the enclosing of rabbits made easy – no walls, hedges or fences were required. Many of the rabbit islands were very successful and their history and the effects of isolation on a rabbit population have been the subject of numerous studies (particularly see R M Lockley *The Private Life of the Rabbit 1954).*

Hutches

As we have seen some kind of cage or hutch has been used to confine rabbits since the days of the Phoenicians who took them on their sea journeys as a self–replacing source of meat and fur; a practice continued by the Romans, as did almost all the great early Colonisers. The development of the rabbit hutch, the types of hutch required and any special features required will be discussed in some detail later, for now we are concerned with the effects of keeping rabbits in hutches had on domestication.

It is almost certainly in the period following Pope Gregory's Papal Edict of 600 AD that monks, particularly in France, started the process of domesticating the wild rabbit in a combination of rabbit courts and hutches.

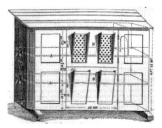

Early rabbit hutch circa 1860

Almost certainly rabbits were selectively bred for size, and even colour, coat or body shape; by keeping them confined in a relatively small area (either a hutch or a rabbit court) then there can be no doubt that some animals would become very large. Thus by breeding many generations of large rabbits to large rabbits it is feasible to imagine a steady increase in size and weight from the 3 pound wild rabbit to the 10, 15 or even 20 pounds of some of the modern breeds. Similarly the early keepers of rabbits may well have seen genetic mutations appearing in their stock and decided to keep a mutation that appealed to them and thus breed from that mutation into future stock.

There can be little doubt that the enclosing of rabbits in Warrens, Gardens or Courts, Islands and Hutches over the last two thousand years has been responsible not only for the taming of the wild rabbit but also for the characteristics that we recognise the individual breeds by today – size, weight, colour, pattern, body type, fur properties, character and eating habits.

2 • Buying Your Rabbit

A Blue Rex – a medium size rabbit.

Netherland Dwarf – a small rabbit.

We have all heard the slogan 'A Dog is for Life, not just for Christmas', obviously this applies equally to rabbits, they are a 365 days a year commitment, they must be fed and watered, and as social animals they need regular companionship. They must be kept in a secure environment, protected against outside dangers and contained to prevent them escaping. You must ask yourself 'is your life style ready to accept another member of the family that can be given the time and affection it deserves?'

When buying a rabbit you must make some big decisions before you even approach a pet shop or rabbit breeder. Firstly you must decide which breed will best suit your lifestyle. There is a vast difference between a Miniature Lop that will only weigh about 3lb 8ozs at adulthood and a Continental Giant that may well have an adult weight of about 20lbs. If you want to show your rabbit then you should really visit some shows (see www.thebrc.org for shows in your area) and look at all the different breeds so you know what the alternatives are, it is there that you can talk to exhibitors and breeders. You will find that the vast majority of breeders will only be too happy to speak to you about their breed.

What sex of rabbit do you want? If you intend to keep your rabbit as a pet then you must consider the physical and temperamental differences. Generally speaking, bucks make better pets as they are usually more playful and have more character, the downside of a pet buck is that some become 'sprayers' as they

*Talk to exhibitors and breeders at local shows so that you know what the alternatives
are before you choose your rabbit.*

A Doe

A Buck

mature sexually and this can be quite unpleasant, especially if it is a child's pet. However, having the buck castrated can usually stop him 'spraying'. Whilst many does grow into affectionate adults there will be times when she will become quite grumpy and start nest building, it is not uncommon for them to bite the hand that feeds them at this time. It is in every doe's nature to produce young and if you do not intend breeding from her then it is perhaps best that you have her neutered (make sure that you use a Veterinary surgeon who is experienced in rabbit surgery) or buy a buck rather than a doe.

If you intend to show your rabbit then you should be aware that, generally speaking, only buck Lops and Fancy rabbits are shown as adults (Fur and Rex adult does are shown), either bucks or does may be shown in the young stock category which is under five months in most breeds.

If you are going to show your rabbit then it must be properly prepared for each show. This will mean turning it upside down to groom the underneath and clean the feet, a task that is considerably easier on the Miniature Lop than it is for any of the Giant breeds.

Large rabbits need large hutches; large hutches require a lot of bedding and generate a lot of waste that you must dispose of. You must have a regular supply of food,although this is not such a problem these days because most Supermarkets sell rabbit food and they are open seven days a week.

Whether you want your rabbit as a pet or for showing and breeding purposes you want a healthy specimen that is not carrying disease or genetic problems and the only way to do this is to buy from a reputable source. All pet shops that sell live animals (including rabbits) in Britain must hold a licence from their Local Council. To gain the licence, at least one member of staff must hold a Certificate in Small Animal Care and their premises will be checked annually by the Licensing Officer to ensure that they are of an acceptable standard. This should guarantee that any animal you buy from a Licensed Pet Shop has been kept in satisfactory conditions, by staff who know how to care for small animals.

Similarly choose a British Rabbit Council registered breeder (see the BRC website for a

ABOVE AND BELOW Pet rabbits for sale in a pet shop.

list of breeders) who is required to sell only healthy stock.

If you intend to buy from a breeder insist on visiting their rabbitry. The breeder must keep their stock in sanitary conditions and any breeder that values their stock will take pride in their rabbitry. A filthy, untidy rabbitry indicates poor stockmanship and should be avoided. Similarly anyone selling rabbits cheaply and cannot sex them or handle them correctly should be avoided.

A genuine breeder who takes pride in their animals will easily be spotted, they will talk freely and knowledgably, they will handle their stock in a kind manner that shows respect for the animal. However there is a lot more to look for, but because rabbits are naturally so appealing it is easy to be taken in by anyone selling a cute looking young rabbit. Please remember that buying rabbits from anyone who is less than reputable is only perpetuating their trade and buying in trouble for the future. The guidelines that follow are intended to make sure that you buy a healthy animal that has a pleasant demeanour that will not only give you years of happiness, but also lead a happy and healthy life.

Buying from a Breeder

Wherever you buy your rabbit from you must ensure that it is 100% healthy, do not even entertain any rabbit that is showing even the slightest signs of any illness. Mentally prepare yourself a checklist; this is similar to what every judge does with every rabbit he picks up on the

Buying from a Breeder

1 Only buy through a reputable breeder. You can find the breeders in your area by contacting the British Rabbit Council or visiting their website or by visiting local rabbit shows. However, the fact that someone is exhibiting at a show or is a member of the BRC is not in itself a guarantee that they are reputable.

2 Visit the rabbitry; this is most important, as it is only in the rabbitry that you will see how the rabbits are kept. The rabbitry should be well managed and clean with rabbits kept singly in large spacious cages. Rabbits are inquisitive and they should come to the front of the cage when you approach it, not cower in a corner at the back.

3 There should be a quarantine section separate from the main rabbitry. No matter how good a rabbitry is, there should be somewhere to isolate a new rabbit coming in or one showing any signs of illness. If there is no such isolation area then you must assume that all rabbits are kept together whether healthy or not, and this is not a sign of good management.

4 Does the breeder advertise his stud bucks for use to other breeders, if so then you should clearly see these stud animals kept permanently isolated from the rest of the stock.

5 You should ask to see and if possible handle the parents of the rabbit you are intending to buy. If they are not of a pleasant disposition then ask yourself what your little bundle of fluff might grow up to be like?

A typical rabbit breeders 'shed'.

show bench. You may think when watching an experienced judge that he couldn't possibly check all these points in such a short space of time, but he does, albeit very quickly and very skilfully. If you feel confident enough to carry out the physical checks yourself ask the pet shop owner or breeder if they mind you handling the rabbit and checking it over. However if you do not feel confident enough to do so yourself you could ask the seller to show you each of the following points. If these checks are not carried out with both you and the owner present then you can only rely on the owner's honesty and will not have any recourse should something turn out to be other than you had been lead to expect. So either yourself, or the seller with you watching, should carry out a Rabbit Health Check.

Colour and Pattern If you intend to show at BRC supported shows or breed from the rabbit then carefully check that its colour and pattern is as it should be. You may have to study the Breeds Standard (on the British Rabbit Council website) because any rabbit that doesn't have the correct colour or pattern will never win at BRC supported shows, although it may still do well in local pet shows. Colour is

Rabbit Health Check

Start at the front of the rabbit and work towards the back end checking all of the following:

Nose should be clear and dry with no discharge.

Teeth should be clean and white, the top teeth should just overlap the bottom ones, do not be fobbed off if the teeth meet and the breeder tells you that they will come right as they grow older – they won't.

Eyes should be clear and bright with no discharge of any kind; if the third eyelid (in the front corner of the eye) is out it is a sign of stress, ask yourself why is it stressed – lack of handling usually.

Ears there should be no damage to the ears, most nicks or cuts in ears do not heal over completely. The ear should be clean and free from any waxing or sign of disease. For any of the lop-eared rabbits if the ears are not set correctly (i.e. hanging close to the cheeks) there really is no simple answer, if the rabbit has enough width across the skull then they may well descend to the correct position in time, but similarly they may not. Again a good look at both parents should tell what is likely to happen.

Front and Back legs should be straight and strong. Turn the rabbit over on its back and look at the front feet, they should be clean, if the babies have been raised in good conditions. The **pads** should be well furred. Check the inside of the front legs for any matting, rabbits use the inside of their front legs to wipe their noses, so any matting may indicate some nasal discharge. Check the **nails**, look for white toe nails, in a coloured rabbit this is a fault and if you intend to show or breed from the rabbit then it must be discounted, because it is an inherited trait and will therefore be passed on to its progeny. Has it got all its toes and a **dewclaw** with no deformities? Check the young rabbit's **back legs and feet** with it lying on its back in your hand then the back legs should lie parallel to the body, check the toes and toe nails as for the front feet.

The genitals should be clean and free from any signs of disease. This is probably the first place you will see signs of general ill health.

Sit the rabbit back on its feet.

Run your hands over its back, with your fingers feel along the ribs and up into the groin, there should be no lumps or irregularities, look especially for a hernia, a small pea-like lump in the middle of the stomach. Check the coat for bald patches or any infestation, rabbit fleas are not uncommon and can usually be seen in the very thin fur around the ears or on the belly.

The tail should be straight with no kinks or breaks in it, run your fingers carefully up the tail and check for any irregularities.

A healthy rabbit enjoys a run in the garden.

certainly very difficult to assess in a youngster and it is probably the one facet of the rabbit that you are going to have to trust the breeder's word on.

Rings If you intend to show the rabbit at BRC supported shows it must have a British Rabbit Council ring on one of its back legs. It is the breeder's responsibility to fit the appropriate ring; it is against BRC rules for you to fit a ring to a rabbit that you have not bred. But do check that the ring is the correct letter for the breed (see appropriate Breed Standard) and is for the correct year. If you are buying a 'rung'

A well-marked butterfly Mini Lop.

A judge checks a rabbit's BRC ring.

rabbit then the breeder must give you a signed Transfer Card. When you have completed the Transfer Card you should send it, with the appropriate fee, to the BRC to have the registration transferred to your name.

Showing If you are purchasing the rabbit with a view to showing it then you should have studied the appropriate Breed Standard before going to see the rabbit. It is also worthwhile spending some time at a show studying the winners; try to fix the look of the winners in your mind. When you are in the breeder's rabbitry ask if you can 'pose' the rabbit (sit it in position as it would be on the show bench) and try to assess its qualities. This is not easy, especially if you have an experienced breeder breathing down your neck, but do not worry because it is exactly what they would do if they were looking at a rabbit with a view to buying it. No breeder is going to sell you his best rabbit, he has bred that for himself, but you must be ruthless in your decision, because soft heartedness means that you will be stuck with a rabbit that never even gets placed. All rabbits go through a gangly stage, which is the period of maximum bone growth, from about 6 weeks to about 14 weeks and whilst they may look like a miniature version of the adult when about 4 weeks old, the period of bone growth is not yet complete. This must therefore be taken into consideration and makes the selecting of a potential winner all the more difficult.

Age It is against British Rabbit Council rules

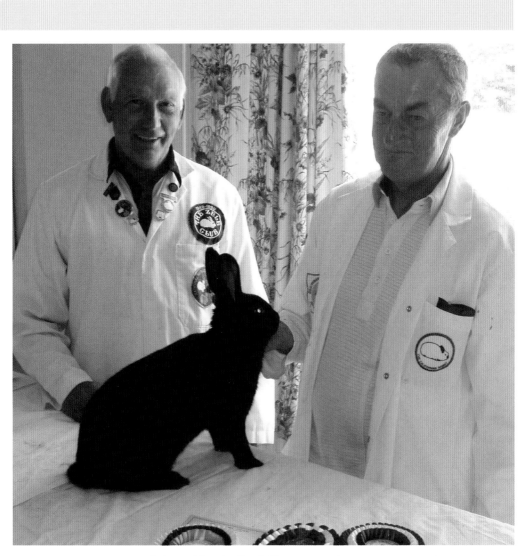

Judge and Breeder, Best in Show – a proud moment

for a breeder to sell a baby rabbit under the age of 8 weeks, however even at 8 weeks old the kits are susceptible to stress related disorders. It is best not to buy a rabbit until it is about 12–14 weeks old, by which time it will be past the danger period for stress related disorders and should make an illness free transfer to your rabbitry. Be very wary of shops or breeders that try to sell very young rabbits, they may look cute but when they are at this age they can develop gastric troubles that can be fatal.

Food The seller (pet shop or breeder) should supply you with at least enough food for the rabbit for one week. This will allow you to gradually mix your chosen food in with what the rabbit is used to eating, so that the transition does not bring on a stomach upset.

Grooming If you have not groomed or cut the nails on the breed of rabbit you are buying get the seller to show you how to do it. There is considerable skill in grooming a longhaired rabbit, if you are not going to have the time or patience to groom on a regular basis then you should avoid the longhaired breeds. Similarly turning a full-grown French Lop over to cut its nails is not for the faint hearted. Cutting a rabbit's nails is not difficult and is a skill that every owner must learn.

Temperament can be very difficult to assess in a fluffy young rabbit, as almost without exception they are all beautiful, loving and cute when young. So what can you do to assess the future temperament of the baby you wish to purchase? First of all, the older the kit is, the more likely it is that any behaviour problem will show itself. By the age of about 14 weeks then the young rabbit can be compared to a teenager, it is at this age that undesirable traits are likely to manifest themselves. So if you buy a very young rabbit, between 8 and 14 weeks then you really have no clue to future behaviour other than assessing the parent's temperament and watching the way the seller handles their stock.

Rabbits that have been well handled from a very young age by an experienced breeder will invariable develop into loving sociable adults.

The process of choosing a young rabbit, whether it is for a pet or for showing, is very important. Of course, most sellers of rabbits are people who love their rabbits and do everything they can to breed and sell healthy specimens, unfortunately, as in most hobbies; there are people out there who are out to con you. You cannot be too careful, as your baby rabbit may well live for up to ten years, so take your time making your choice. Rabbits are beautiful animals and the greatest pitfall is that they are exceptionally cute when young, so do not let your heart rule your head. If you want your rabbit as a pet you simply want a healthy animal, if you want it for showing you want a healthy rabbit that exhibits the qualities required by the Breed Standard.

There are many rabbit rescue centres throughout the country such as this one, the Greenwich Rabbit Rescue centre in London.

Rabbit Re-Homing and Rescue Centres

Unfortunately many, far too many, rabbits become unwanted for a variety of reasons and wind up in rabbit rescue centres. Of course one of the good traits in our society is that there are always caring individuals who will, for no financial reward, look after these abandoned creatures. If you are looking for a rabbit as a pet then you may be able to find it in your heart to adopt a rabbit from a rescue centre. It will be healthy, the rescue centres would not put a sick animal up for re-homing, it may well be neutered/castrated already and you may be asked to contribute towards the costs of vaccinations for the rabbit. But you will be giving a rabbit that did not get the best start in life a second chance and freeing up a space in the rescue centre for another unwanted rabbit to be rescued.

There are rescue centres throughout the country and many have website, one such centre is the Greenwich Rabbit Rescue (www.greenwichrabbitrescue.com), take a look at the website, it has links to many other rescue centres on it, you may be able to give one of their rescue rabbits a home.

27

3 • Feeding Your Rabbit

Rabbits are HERBIVORES; their diet consists almost entirely of vegetable matter. In the wild, herbivores (including rabbits) spend much of their time feeding or grazing and our domesticated rabbits need the activity of feeding over a long period of each day. To achieve this long eating period we must feed a balanced and varied diet of:

The Essential Rabbit Diet

- Concentrated rabbit pellets or a specially prepared rabbit mix,
- Fresh, raw fruit or vegetables
- Sweet meadow hay
- Fresh, clean water available at all times

Whilst it is quite possible to make up your own feed for your rabbit using rolled oats, bran, fish meal or soya flour, linseed cake and maize meal, really good commercially produced rabbit feeds are readily available and cheap, so there is really little point. Experts have researched the correct balance of proteins, fats, carbohydrates and vitamins and minerals that a rabbit should have in its diet and these are combined in commercially available rabbit feeds, so unless you are an animal nutritionist it really is not worthwhile creating your own feeds.

In a good pet shop you will find an array of different rabbit feed and it will be up to you to decide which one to give to your rabbit. There are basically two types of rabbit feed,

'Rabbit Pellets' and 'Rabbit Mix'. Rabbit pellets are just that, they are a uniform brown in colour and contain all the required nutrients for the rabbit's diet; they are usually packaged in a plain brown bag. A rabbit mix has been made to look attractive, with a variety of grains and vegetables in a variety of colours, usually attractively packaged with pictures of cute little bunnies. Most rabbit breeders and exhibitors in Britain feed rabbit pellets, whilst most pet rabbit owners feed rabbit mixes.

A plastic gravity feed bin allows the rabbit to feed on demand and avoids food being left on the hutch floor where it can become contaminated. The bin is easily kept clean.

Why should this be? It would be easy to say that it is mainly down to marketing; pellets look unattractive and boring whilst many of the 'mixes' look and even smell really nice. This defines the historic difference between breeders and pet owners in Britain, whereas in the USA 90% of all rabbits are fed on pellets. In reality it really does not matter how the food is presented to the rabbit so long as it is given all the nutrients it requires and it eats them all. And here lies the problem with 'mixes', which allow the rabbit to eat selectively, missing vital nutrients, whilst with pellets it is guaranteed that the rabbit gets the complete diet it requires.

In fact it is the breakdown of the content of the food that is far more important than its presentation method. It is normal to feed high protein (16–18%) food to rabbits that have a

Rabbit pellets

Rabbit mix

29

demanding lifestyle i.e. show rabbits, breeding does, stud bucks whereas the more sedentary rabbit i.e. pets, resting or retired breeding does are fed on a low protein (12–14%) diet. If your rabbit is a selective eater and leaves certain items in a rabbit mix then perhaps it would be best to feed it on pellets, otherwise a commercially marketed rabbit mix with a protein level of between 12–14% will be quite adequate to form the basis of the diet.

You can however, be creative in the fresh fruit and vegetables that you supplement the diet with. Feed only a little each day of what is in season or you have left over. Any fruit or vegetables that you feed your rabbit must be fresh and clean. Stale, rotten or dirty left over fruit and vegetables are best consigned to the compost heap, not fed to your rabbit because their stomachs are quite delicate and very easily upset. Never feed greens to rabbits under 12 weeks of age because their stomachs are not developed enough to digest them.

Hay of the very best quality is a vital ingredient of a rabbit's diet; chewing the long strands of hay grinds their teeth keeping them short and healthy, whilst the absorption of the roughage is a vital part of the rabbit's digestive system, added to this is the fact that it takes them a long time to 'chew' the hay which is very similar to their 'grazing' in the wild and prevents them getting bored. Fresh, sweet (yes, it should actually smell quite sweet) hay should be placed in a hayrack securely mounted on the wall of the rabbit's hutch so that it can feed whenever it feels like it throughout the waking day.

The fourth and final vital element of the rabbits diet is fresh water which should be available at all times, preferably through a drip-feed bottle mounted through the wire mesh on the front of the cage.

Food hygiene is just as important with your rabbit's food as it is with your own food.

- Fresh food must be given everyday and any food leftover from the previous day should be removed and disposed of.

Fruit and Vegetables that Rabbits Particularly Like

- Apples
- Brussels Sprouts
- Cabbage
- Carrots
- Cauliflower
- Celery
- Chicory
- Kale
- Lettuce (they like it but it is not particularly good for them)
- Parsnip
- Pears
- Peas and their pods
- Spinach
- Swede
- Turnip

A Rex rabbit enjoys his hay from a hay rack.

Drinking from a bowl.

- Vegetables and fruit that get dropped on the hutch floor will almost certainly become contaminated and will not be eaten by the rabbit therefore they should be removed to the compost heap.
- All food bowls should be thoroughly washed on a regular basis.
- Water bottles should be kept scrupulously clean and refilled daily.
- Hay should be provided in a hayrack to

prevent it being trampled into the bedding.

How Much to Feed and When

Rabbits are creatures of habit, consequently the 'when' is just as important as the 'how much'. You can feed your rabbit once, twice or even three times a day; twice is probably the most popular and most 'normal' for the majority of rabbits.

The daily ration of dry pellets or rabbit mix

A commercially available drinking bottle which has a metal cover over the screw cap to avoid chewing damage, flexible metal straps and a clip to attach to the mesh in the hutch and a yellow warning float to a indicate when the water level drops to a minimum.

TIP: To clean the inside of a water bottle

1 Take top off of the bottle and put ½" of warm water in it.
2 Place a length of chain – sink plug chain is ideal – in the bottle.
3 Place thumb over top of bottle.
4 Shake vigorously.
5 Empty water and chain out of bottle
6 Rinse thoroughly with clean water
7 Refill and replace top.

Water bottle clipped to outside of cage.

can be split in two, with half given in the morning and the other half at night, similarly split the hay ration into two feeds. Vegetables may be given at lunchtime, to break the day up if you are going to be around every lunchtime, otherwise you may decide to give the vegetables with the morning feed. To keep to a routine of feeding is more important than what you give or when you give. Work out feeding times to suit your lifestyle and stick to them.

It is quite difficult to work out exactly how much pellet or rabbit mix to give your rabbit.

You can

1 Stick to the recommended quantities for the breed, i.e. 2oz of pellets per day for a Mini Lop. But just like humans, individual rabbit's metabolisms vary, some will be quite active and require a lot of food whereas a lazy rabbit will not need so much.

TIP: To measure the food

Once you have calculated your rabbit's ration per meal, find a suitable container i.e. a yogurt pot, mark a line on it corresponding to the ration per meal and then just use the pot to scoop out the same ration every time

Daily rations

2 Ask the breeder what they feed their adults on and stick to the same. Probably quite a sound method, but then do you eat the same as your mother or father?

3 The trial and reduce method. A rabbit should eat its dry ration (pellets or rabbit mix) within an hour of being fed. Using the recommended for breed (1 above) watch to see how long it takes your rabbit to empty its bowl. If it does not empty the bowl within the hour then slightly reduce the ration, if the rabbit dives at the bowl and empties it within minutes then add a little until the correct amount is found.

Your rabbit's rations may have to be adjusted throughout the year. In summer you may let it out to roam in the garden where, although it is grazing on your grass (and maybe anything else that is growing), it is getting a lot more exercise and therefore may need more feed. In winter, although 'confined to quarters' for longer period, it may need more to eat to generate heat to combat the effects of the cold.

TIP: To prevent obesity

Decrease food quantity as your rabbit ages. Prevent obesity at all cost; it is a killer in rabbits as in humans

TIP: Tasty treat

Keep leftover brown bread (white will not do) and when you take your dinner out of the oven put the bread on a rack in the hot, but cooling, oven. It will bake to the tastiest treat that you could possibly give your rabbit. They absolutely love it.

So yes, be sensible and try and feed the same everyday but at the same time be prepared to be flexible.

Treats

The feeding of treats to rabbits over and above the daily ration is a highly contentious subject.

What will you use as a treat? Pet Shops have many propriety brands of rabbit treats and of course, just like giving your children sweets, there is nothing wrong with these in moderation. But it could just as easily be a tasty leaf picked from the garden or my rabbit's favourite treat – baked dry brown bread.

Wild and Garden Plants

Rabbits will relish many of the wild plants collected from the countryside, such as avens, agrimony, bramble or blackberry, burnet, broom, coltsfoot, comfrey, cow parsnip, dock, fat hen, goose grass, groundsel, heather, hedge parsley, knapweed, nettles, shepherd's

Green leaves are a tasty treat for this Lop.

purse and sow thistle, trefoil, vetches and yarrow. They also love to graze grass and the weeds in it like plantains, chickweed, dandelion, and clover. There are whole books devoted to the plants that you can and cannot feed your rabbit but in the urban society in which we live today can you actually recognise all the wild plants? Once you have recognized them can you guarantee that they are not contaminated with weed killers, fertilizers, car fumes or even other animals (especially dogs and cats) fouling? Unless you are a real country person who knows your plants and is happy that they are unpolluted then perhaps it is better to make the 'green' part of your rabbit's diet up from vegetable leftovers and fruit.

Feeding Do's

- Feed at the same time every day
- Remove any uneaten food from the day before
- Wash fruit and vegetables before feeding
- Give raw, fresh vegetables – not cooked or frozen
- A mixture of vegetables is better than a lot of one kind
- Make sure fresh hay is always available, in hay rack
- Fresh clean water must be available at all times
- Introduce any new kind of food gradually
- Keep all rabbit food in a vermin-free container

Rabbit Likes

VEGETABLES	FRUIT
Beetroot	Grapes
Chicory	Apples
Carrots	Pears
Cabbage	Banana
Jerusalem Artichokes	Strawberry leaves
Kohl Rabi	Raspberry leaves
Kales	
Cauliflower	
Lettuce	
Sunflowers	
Swedes	

Feeding Don'ts

- Don't make sudden changes to the diet
- Don't feed frosted or stale green food or roots
- Don't gather green food from areas where it could have been fouled
- Don't gather green food from beside busy roads
- Don't leave grass or greens in a heap where they can start to 'heat up'
- Don't feed from the hutch floor where food can become contaminated

4 • Housing Your Rabbit

The Essentials of Good Rabbit Housing

- Provide space for the rabbit to live and exercise
- Durability to keep the rabbit comfortable in all weathers
- Robust construction to prevent the rabbit destroying it
- Keep the rabbit in hygienic conditions
- Keep the rabbit secure and prevent escape
- Keep the rabbit safe from predators

Never has a popular phrase been more apposite than 'buy in haste, regret at your leisure' when talking about the purchasing of rabbit housing. There are so many hutches and runs to choose from and they vary from the Penthouse Suite to a drafty shack. Buy the biggest and best that you can afford, your initial outlay will be repaid in the long run and your rabbit will thank you for it.

Space for the rabbit to Live and Exercise

There is no specific size requirement laid down for a rabbit hutch as each breed varies in shape and size, and more than one 'may' be kept in the same hutch.

Wild rabbits spend nearly two-thirds of their day underground in cramped burrows; similarly our domestic rabbits spend much of their day 'resting'. It is not always the size of the hutch

that is as important as the size of the exercise area and the amount of time the rabbit has access to it. Bearing this in mind it is probably best to have a hutch with a run permanently attached.

Durability to survive the weather

Whilst we in Great Britain do not suffer the extremes of weather that many countries do, our outdoor rabbit hutch is going to have to withstand quite a battering in the course of its lifetime and obviously we would like the hutch to have as long a life as possible. A poorly

TIP: Follow the rules

The Welfare Livestock Regulations (1994) state that 'Any hutches or cages where rabbits are kept shall be (a) of sufficient size to allow the rabbits to move around and to feed and drink without difficulty and to enable all the rabbits kept in them to lie on their sides at the same time; and (b) of sufficient height to allow the rabbits to sit upright on all four feet without their ears touching the top of the cage.'
'Where any rabbits are kept in any accommodation that is exposed to the weather, suitable steps shall be taken so as to ensure that the rabbits have access to shelter from the action of the weather (including direct sunlight).'

constructed plywood hutch is clearly not going to last long nor is it probably going to keep the rabbit warm and dry. An outdoor hutch should be constructed using heavy-duty tongue and groove timber that is either treated with a non-poisonous wood preservative or covered in a waterproof material, like roofing felt.

Naturally you want your rabbit to have plenty of room and to be comfortable in its hutch but the main function of the hutch is to allow the rabbit to escape from the worst of the weather. In the wild rabbits simply go down

A really big traditional hutch by Forsham Cottage Arks.

Morant Run with shelter at one end.

A delux hutch

into their burrows to avoid weather that does not suit them. Your rabbit's hutch should have an area where the rabbit can shelter from the wind and rain; rabbits do not mind the cold, in fact many thrive in the coldness of winter, but they cannot tolerate damp. Whilst a good hutch will have an enclosed sleeping area where a rabbit can shelter from extremely high or low temperatures, high winds or driving rain, many hutches have either shutters (with ventilation holes) or drop down covers that can be put in place during the worst of the weather.

Robustness to prevent rabbit damage

Rabbits chew. In the wild they are used to chewing through tree roots that get in their way in the burrow. In a hutch they are highly likely to chew any wooden surface they can get their teeth around. The best way to prevent them damaging their hutches like this is to prevent boredom by providing plenty of distractions; exercise areas with plenty of stimulating things to do and of course plenty of companionship – even if it is human companionship it will help reduce the damage. But it is another case for a really robust hutch that will stand up to what can be pretty hard treatment.

In most hutches it is the flooring that will fail first. The wood used to make the floor of the rabbit hutch should be at least a quarter of an inch (6mm) thick and it should be treated with an animal friendly sealant and the edges should be glued as well as nailed to prevent seepage. Regular cleaning of the 'dirty corner',

or even better, training the rabbit to use a litter tray will prevent a lot of 'urine damage' to the floor.

Keep the rabbit in hygienic conditions

The Allotments Act (1950) and The Environmental Protection Act (1990) both require rabbits to be kept in a 'sanitary condition' and in 'a structure that is visually attractive'. Unless you decide to build your rabbit's hutch yourself and your skills are somewhat lacking then most shop bought hutches would probably be classed as visually attractive.

It is important that the design of the hutch is such that it is easy for the owner to reach every corner during cleaning. The wood should be treated in such a way as to prevent urine and faeces seeping into the wood.

By raising the hutch at least one to two feet (30.5 – 61cms) above the ground and keeping it at least nine inches (25cms) away from the wall air is able to circulate around the hutch aiding ventilation and the drying of any damp wood. Whilst rabbits don't like damp conditions neither does the wood the hutch is built of; damp wood rots and allows pathogens to build up.

Keep the rabbit secure

Surely there could be few worse shocks than to go out to your rabbit in the morning and find the hutch door open and your rabbit gone! A hutch must be secure; it must keep your rabbit enclosed and safe.

All door catches on the hutch must be able to be secured so that a rabbit getting hold of the inside of the door with its teeth and vigorously shaking it does not allow it to fall open. Most pet rabbits will not survive long in the wild, especially in the winter. The rabbit's hutch is its home and it should be sufficiently strong enough to keep the rabbit enclosed, and safe, whilst it is unattended.

Keep the rabbit safe from predators

Your rabbit's natural reaction to attack is 'fear and flight'; in the wild a rabbit races for its burrow at the first sign of attack. In a hutch the rabbit literally has nowhere to go should it

LEFT Many dogs will live happily with rabbits – but not all of them.

A super hutch with run attached.

Checklist for Garden Rabbit

- Hutch
- Outdoor run – maybe attached to hutch
- Cover for inclement weather
- Wood shavings
- Barley Straw – for bedding
- Ceramic food dishes
- Drip – feed water bottle
- Hayrack
- Sweet Meadow Hay
- Food
- Toys/Chews
- Grooming Kit
- Cleaning out kit – dustpan and brush, scraper, bucket and scrubber

come under attack from a predator, although it can hide in an enclosed sleeping compartment if it has one. A hutch must be strong and secure so that an attacking dog could not knock it over. Catches must be secure so that a cat could not open the hutch and attack the rabbit. Wire mesh should be no more than 1"x ½"

(2.5 x 1.5cms) so that a cat cannot get its paw in through the wire.

Foxes can be persistent trouble makers once they learn where a rabbit lives; even if your hutch is secure a rabbit that is threatened night after night by a hungry fox will suffer from stress and may well even die from the effects of the trauma. If you suspect the presence of a fox the hutch and rabbit should be lifted into a shed for a few nights until the fox has lost interest.

Every effort must be made to keep the rabbit hutch and surrounding area free from rats and mice; vermin will bring disease into your rabbit's hutch but also terrify the rabbit.

Positioning your Rabbit Hutch

Correctly sighting your rabbit's hutch is vitally important. The hutch needs to be in a sheltered position, it should not face the midday sun or the prevailing wind direction and should be close to the house so that all members of the family are encouraged to visit the rabbit and give it the social interaction that it needs.

Healthy rabbits are quite hardy animals and quite tolerant of the cold as long as they are dry. The addition of plenty of clean, dry straw will keep your rabbit quite comfortable on a frosty night. But if the forecast is for wind and rain then the hutch may either have to be moved to a more sheltered spot or a suitably ventilated cover dropped over the front of the hutch.

Sun and heat are far more dangerous to rabbits than cold weather; in the wild rabbits retreat to the coolness of their burrows during the heat of the day but a rabbit 'trapped' in a hutch exposed to the full midday sun may well die of heat exhaustion. There are many ways to overcome the ill effects of the midday sun, but they must be planned before leaving work for the day. The hutch may have to be moved under trees or to a shaded position, temporary shade can be erected, frozen bottles of water put in the hutch for the rabbit to lie against, ceramic tiles placed in the hutch give the rabbit a cool spot to lie on. A hose could be laid to run cold water over the top of the hutch, there is so much that can be done but it does require thought before the event, it is too late when the rabbit is lying on its side panting from heat exhaustion.

House Rabbits

Cages and hutches for house rabbits are widely available in pet shops and superstores; just like outdoor rabbit hutches they vary vastly in quality and price. The House Rabbit Association has advice leaflets on housing a house rabbit to download from their website at www.houserabbit.co.uk.

A small colourful mobile toy helps to keep the hutch-bound rabbit entertained and stimulated.

Rabbits train very easily to use a litter tray

An indoor cage must be carefully sited.

A plastic litter tray is easily kept clean and with odor absorbing litter granules will help to keep the indoor hutch smelling sweet in your home.

Checklist for a House Rabbit

- Purpose built indoor rabbit cage
- Rabbit play pen
- Litter Tray
- Wood shavings
- Drip-feed water bottle
- Ceramic feed bowls
- Hayrack
- Sweet Meadow Hay
- Food
- Toys/Chews
- Grooming Kit
- Cleaning out kit – dustpan and brush, scraper, bucket and scrubber, disinfectant

Sighting of a house rabbit cage is just as important as sighting an outdoor hutch. It must not be in a draught or beside a heater that will cause the temperature to rise and fall as the heater comes on and goes off, beside a window that could trap the rabbit in the midday sun. Whilst you will want your house rabbit to be part of the family activities you do not want the cage in the way where people are constantly tripping over it.

Is your rabbit to live in a house with other pets? If so then its cage should be somewhere where it can have private time away from the other pets when it needs it.

Is your rabbit to live in a house with children? If so then it should not have its cage in a child's (or anyone else's) bedroom – rabbits can be active through the much of the night and very early in the morning.

Puppy pens and child stair gates can be used to allow your rabbit a safe play/exercise area out of their cage yet in the house.

Hygiene will be a very important consideration in a house rabbit's cage; plastic cages are obviously easy to clean but always look for a cage with a deep base unit that will contain the shavings that the rabbit will undoubtedly scratch about in. You do not want to be continually vacuuming shavings out of your carpet.

Rabbits can be trained very easily to use a litter tray that can more conveniently be kept clean and hygienic. Use wood shavings in the litter tray, not cat litter, and position where the rabbit can access it easily.

PART TWO

Keeping Your Rabbit Happy and Healthy

5 • Rabbits: Caring Through the Seasons

Spring

- Check out run, if it has been stored away since last summer. Make any necessary repairs or buy a new one.
- If the weather is dry for a few days let your rabbit out in the run for short periods. Be careful it does not gorge on wet greens and upset its stomach.
- Spring clean hutch on a sunny, warm, dry day.
- Put the rabbit in run or somewhere secure for the day.
- Empty the hutch of all material.
- Check for any repairs that may need doing – carry out repairs.
- Thoroughly scrub inside of the hutch using 'pet' disinfectant.
- Use a blowtorch to scorch inside of hutch, paying particular attention to cracks and joins. This may be quite a dangerous thing

Hutch Scraper

to do and all relevant safety precautions should be taken, if you are unsure then you should find someone to help you who is proficient at using a blowtorch or paint stripper. The advantage of using this method is that you can get right in the cracks and joints in the hutch and destroy any microorganisms that could develop during the heat of the summer.

- Allow to dry completely.
- Replace any damaged or worn equipment – bowl, bottle, hayrack, litter tray, toys or gnawing blocks.
- Replace with fresh bedding and food.
- Replace your rabbit in its hutch.
- Check fly screens/fly protection is in place ready for the summer.
- Put bottles of water in freezer ready for hot

Assemble your cleaning kit before you start.

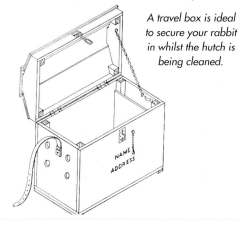

A travel box is ideal to secure your rabbit in whilst the hutch is being cleaned.

summer days.

🐾 Take your rabbit to the vet for a six monthly check and booster vaccinations (Myxomatosis and VHD).

Summer

🐾 Ensure the run and hutch are in a position shaded from full sunlight.

🐾 Put fly screens/fly protection in place.

🐾 Give plenty of exercise – preferably early morning or in the cooler evening.

🐾 Be especially vigilant for diarrhoea – take immediate action to clean your rabbit to avoid flys. See Fly Strike in diseases section.

🐾 Do not leave uneaten food in hutch to rot and attract unwanted microorganisms.

🐾 Watch the daily weather forecast so that you can be prepared on especially hot days to:

- Move hutch to full shade.
- Run water over hutch.
- Place wet towel over door opening.
- Place a frozen brick or bottle of water in hutch for rabbit to lay against.
- Place a ceramic tile in hutch for rabbit to lay on.
- Place a bowl of cool, fresh water in hutch.

🐾 Do not leave the rabbit unattended for lengthy periods, if you must go away then get a neighbour to check it frequently.

🐾 Let the rabbit enjoy a variety of fresh greens that are available at this time of year, it will help build up immunity and strength for the coming winter.

Make sure only fresh greens are left in the rabbit's bowl.

Summer is a good time for a run in the garden.

Hutch fans can help keep rabbit cool during hot weather.

Check the bedding is not damp.

Autumn

🐾 Move hutch to position where it will benefit from any winter sun that is available.

🐾 Make sure new position of hutch is out of prevailing wind and rain

🐾 Check waterproofing on hutch.

🐾 Ensure the hutch stands about 10 inches (25cm) away from any wall to allow air circulation

🐾 Fit storm flap (with ventilation) to hutch.

🐾 Store the run during the winter

🐾 Cold will not be a problem at this time of year but damp will, so make sure your daily routine includes checking the bedding is dry.

🐾 Where do you store your food, hay and straw? – remember vermin are looking for a cosy place to stay for the winter; make sure it will not be in your food or bedding.

🐾 Fireworks seem to go on forever these days and they scare rabbits. You may have to make arrangements to bring your rabbit into the house on nights when the fireworks are particularly bad.

Winter

🐾 Make sure you have a clear dry path to the hutch.

🐾 Rabbits can tolerate the cold but they do not like to be damp so fit a storm flap when weather is really bad to prevent rain or snow getting into the hutch.

🐾 If bedding is kept dry it will not freeze – clean dirty corners and replace bedding frequently.

🐾 Add extra dry straw on particularly cold nights.

🐾 Do not destroy your rabbit's regular feeding routine with 'Christmas treats.' They do not know that it is Christmas and will not thank you for an upset stomach.

🐾 Have a secure box that you can put your rabbit in whilst you clean its hutch. In the summer you may have let it have a run in

While you clean out his hutch, your rabbit can relax.

the garden while you cleaned out, but you may not be able to do the same in the winter if the weather is bad, so it is better to box the rabbit whilst you clean out.

During frosty and freezing weather be sure to check the water bottle frequently especially first thing in the morning as a rabbit cannot drink from a frozen bottle. You can now buy insulators for rabbit bottles but an old sock will also do the trick. Keep a spare bottle in the house so that you can replace a frozen bottle and allow the rabbit to drink.

6 • *Glossary*

Glossary of Rabbit Related Terms

A

Adult Rabbit – a rabbit over 5 months old is considered an adult for show purposes (NOTE this does not mean for breeding purposes).

Adult Coat – a rabbit's mature coat that is produced for the first time when it is between 6–9 months

AC – Any Colour

Ad – Adult

Agouti – the coat pattern found in wild rabbits

Albino – A Red-eyed white rabbit that is recessive to colour, that will always breed true when mated together, but may genetically mask any other colour.

All Rounder Judge – A senior judge who is equally qualified in all breeds

Any Colour – Any colour or pattern that conforms to the colour or pattern of recognised breeds

AOC – Any Other Colour

AOV – Any Other Variety

Arch – gentle curvature of the spine

Arch – the gentle curvature of the spine, best seen by viewing the animal in side profile.

ASS – Adult Stock Show

Astringent – A property of some plants useful in treating scours in that it opposes any laxative effect

AV – Any Variety

B

Baby Coat – the rabbit's early or first coat, usually up to 3–5 months of age

Bagginess – looseness of coat, particularly around the rump of older rabbits

Blue-eyed White

Banding – the hair shaft having various colours, particularly in agouti patterned rabbits

Barred Feet – lighter stripes on coloured feet, a common fault on agouti pattern, chinchilla and fox patterned rabbits

Barrel – length – long and round in the body

Barren, Barrenness – the inability of a doe to bear young, infertility

Base Colour – colour of the hair shaft closest to the body

BEW – Blue-eyed white

BIS (BiS) – Best in Show

Blaze – the white marking running up the nose and between the ears in the Dutch

Bloat – a condition where the stomach and intestines fill up with gas, potentially fatal condition that is extremely hard to cure

Bloom – the vitality and finish of a coat in good condition

Bold Eye – a prominent, full eye – the sign of a healthy rabbit

Bowed Legs – usually seen where the front legs are bent like a 'bow' – curved outwards in the middle

Breeder – the owner of the dam at the time of kindling

Breeder's Class – a class at a show that is confined to exhibitors who bred the exhibit (*see definition above*)

Brindling – coloured or white hairs interspersed in the desired colour, common fault in Sooty Fawns

BRC – British Rabbit Council

The British Rabbit Council logo

Broken Coat – where the coat is adversely affected by moult, exposing the undercoat or new coat coming through

Broken Pattern – a random mixture of an accepted colour on a white base

Broody Doe – a doe ready for mating

Buck – a male rabbit

A Butterfly French Lop

Butterfly Nose-Markings – the coloured butterfly-like pattern on the nose of a butterfly rabbit, exhibition butterflies should have no white on the upper lip and no colour on the lower lip

Butterfly – a very specific pattern that must carry the butterfly-nose-pattern. (see specific Breeds Standard on BRC website)

C

Carriage – The way and style in which a rabbit bears itself, particularly ears in a Lop

Castration – removal of the male organs of reproduction

Challenge Certificate – certificate awarded at a BRC supported show to rabbits of outstanding merit that are registered with the BRC in the name of the exhibitor

Chain – the spots on the sides of an English rabbit running from neck to loin

Charlie – a term applied to a rabbit that is extremely light in colour, usually a butterfly patterned rabbit that has insufficient body markings but usually retains its coloured ears and a 'Charlie Chaplin' moustache instead of the full butterfly-nose-markings. Not a showable pattern in Britain.

BRC Challenge Certificate

Cheeks – rounded area between eyes and jaw

Cheek Spots – a single spot at the side of the eye in English rabbits

Chest – the front of the rabbit between the

Cheek Spots and Chain on an English rabbit.

forelegs and the chin

Chinchillation – the elimination of yellow from the coat as in Chinchillas. Agouti or wild colour is the opposite.

Chopped – applied to type, having the rump cut off abruptly and falling vertically to the tail instead of being rounded

Clean Cut – the line of demarcation between markings being clear, with no tendency of one colour to 'run' into another

Cobby – a short and stocky body type which is close coupled and very compact

Condition – the physical state of the rabbit with reference to its health

Cowhocks – hocks that are bent inwards causing the feet to turn outwards

Crock – a pot or container, ideally ceramic, for holding the rabbit's feed

Cross-Breeding – the breeding together of two different breeds or colours of rabbit

Chinchillation

Dewlap – pouch of loose skin under neck

D

Dam – the mother of a litter

Proud mum

Definition – in Chinchilla and Agouti patterned rabbits the clear line of demarcation between the pearling and the undercolour

Density – the number of hairs per square inch on the skin. Essential in all the Fur breeds.

Dewlap – the pouch of loose skin under the neck, usually seen in mature does

Diploma – certificate awarded at BRC supported shows to Best in Show or Best in Section

Doe – female rabbit

Dewclaw – an extra toe on the inside of the front legs

Drags – intrusion of colour into white area areas of fur

E

Ear Label – a small sticky label bearing the rabbit's pen number at a show

Ear Lacing – a coloured line of fur that outlines the sides and tips of the ear.

Eye Circle – The contrasting colour circle of fur next to the eye

Eye Stain – circle of colour around the eyes of Himalayans, a fault

F

Fancier/The Fancy – A member of the (rabbit) Fancy
OED definition – *'the art or practice of breeding animals so as to develop particular points'*

Fancy Section – one of the four divisions used by the BRC, Fancy rabbits are purely show rabbits i.e. Poles, Netherland Dwarfs and Tans

Feathering – a division of white and colour in a pattern that is irregular or lacking in clear definition

Fine Boned – a term used to describe a

A Pole is said to be 'Fine Boned'.

Fly Back – the coat when stroked against the lie 'flies back' the opposite of a 'roll back' coat. Fly back is the desired coat in some breeds i.e. Poles.

Fore Feet – front feet

Foster Mother – a doe used in the rearing of another doe's litter

Foreign Colour – any colour of fur, nails or eyes differing from that required by the breed standard

Frosty Nose – the sprinkling of hair found on the nose of some tan- patterned breeds especially Foxes, which gives a frosted appearance. It is a fault.

rabbit's bone structure, a Pole is said to be 'fine boned'

Finish – the desired degree of perfection in condition of coat – a finished rabbit

Firm Condition – the desired condition where the skeleton is well covered with firm flesh

First Cross (F1) – the immediate offspring of two pure breeds mated together

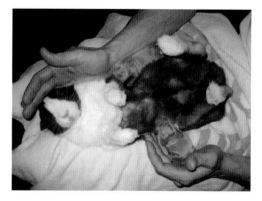

Foster Mother – a Dutch doe feeding young English Lops.

Full Coat – adult coat free from moult – a highly desirable condition

G

Gestation – the period of pregnancy. Usually between 30–32 days.

Ghost – a very light chinchilla with wide pearling and little or no undercolour

Glossy – a bright coat that reflects the light, as opposed to dull and lifeless appearance of the fur

Groin – the area between the hind legs and the belly

Guard Hairs – the longer and stronger hairs found in the coat; the presence of guard hairs is particularly important in the roll back coat

H

Hock – the last joint on a hind leg

Herringbone – the saddle running down the back of an English resembling the backbone of a herring

I

Inbreeding – the mating together of very close relations such as father and daughter, mother and son, brother and sister

In Kindle – pregnant doe

Intermediate Coat – the coat prior to the full adult coat that generally appears about 4–5½ months old

Iris – the coloured portion of the eye, surrounding the pupil

Herringbone clearly visible on this Tortoiseshell English

A new born litter

K

Kindling – the birth of a litter

L

Lactating – the production of milk by a doe

Line Breeding – the mating together of rabbits of the same strain, but not so close as that of inbreeding

Litter – the youngsters born from a single pregnancy

Lop Ear – pendulous ears, carried below horizontal rather than upright

M

Malocclusion – teeth having the lower incisors extending in front of the upper incisors or meeting with no overlap. This condition may be hereditary and maloccluded rabbits should not be bred from.

Mandolin – having the appearance of a mandolin laid face down. Body arch starting at the back of the shoulders rather than the nape of the neck.

Marked Rabbit – a scab, scar or mark (but specifically not a vaccine mark), usually damage, a deformity or mutilation that identifies a rabbit. A disqualification at a BRC show.

Mask – the shadings on the face of a rabbit

Matted – wool or fur tangled in a thick mass, especially in the longhaired breeds

Mealy Colour – a lighter shade of the required colour that gives an almost speckled appearance and is undesirable

Moult – the casting of one coat and the growth of new fur

Judging a class of young English Lops at an agricultural show.

Mutation – the sudden origin of an entirely new type such as the first Rex

Muzzle – the lower part of the face and nose

Myxomatosis [myxie]– disease introduced by farmers to control wild populations of rabbits can be prevented in domestic rabbits by regular vaccination

O

Open Coat – coat lacks the ability to return to its natural position when stroked towards the head

Ovary – the female organ of reproduction

Outcrossing – breeding unrelated rabbits or lines within the same breed

P

Parasite – another organism that lives on, or within, the host animal. Examples are mange, mites, lice and fleas.

Pearling – the lighter band of colour in the chinchilla coat which comes next to the undercoat

Pea Spots – two spots at the root of the ears when viewed from the front, in 'tan' patterned varieties

Pedigree – the record of parentage, in rabbits this is not an officially issued document, anyone can write a pedigree for a rabbit just to record its parentage

Pendant Ears – hanging ears – essential in Lops

Points – the coloured extremities of the rabbit.

Points – the coloured extremities of the rabbit e.g. in Himalayans

Pot Belly – enlarged stomach due to fermentation of food causing the formation of gases. Usually due to faulty feeding.

Pseudo Pregnancy (False Pregnancy) – a doe exhibiting all the signs of pregnancy (including nesting) but producing no young

Putty Nose – white spot on the nose extremity, a disqualification in BRC show rabbits

R

Racy – a derogatory term meaning long in the body and lacking breadth, especially in the shoulders

Rat Faced – narrow skull and head

REW – Red-eyed white

Ring – metal band, sold by the BRC to paid-up members only and fitted to one of the rear legs of the rabbit. All rabbits (except tattooed imports) must be fitted with a ring when young in order for them to be shown later in their lives.

A judge checks the BRC Ring.

Roll-Back Coat – a gradual return to the normal position of the fur when stroked from the rump to the shoulders, the kind of coat desired in many breeds

Roman Nose – a nose whose bridge is so comparatively high as to form a slightly convex line from the forehead to nose tip. An especially pronounced feature in the English Lop.

Rump – the hindquarters of the rabbit

Run (1) – the intrusion of white colour into a coloured marked area on a marked breed

Run (2) – an exercise area, usually may from wire netting, for the rabbit; the run may be either attached permanently to the rabbit's hutch or be detached.

This hutch has an exercise run downstairs.

Rusty Colour – as applied to black or blue rabbits, rusty tinge that can be caused by exposure to sunlight, crossbreeding or at certain stages of the moult. Undesirable.

S

Saddle – the whole upper portion of the back

Scours – diarrhoea

Screw Tail – tail twisted to one side, particularly a problem in the long-tailed breeds e.g. Hares

Scut – a tail

Shaded Pattern – Smoke Pearl Netherland Dwarf.

Self – the rabbit being the same colour all over. Undercolour is usually paler. Examples are REW, BEW, Black, Blue, Brown (Chocolate), and Lilac.

Shaded Pattern – the pattern found in Siamese Sable, Siamese Smokes, Seal Points and Sooty Fawns

Shadings – variation in shades from darker on the saddle to lighter on the sides, especially in sables and smokes

Shape – the general conformation of a rabbit's overall appearance, as shown by body structure, Synonym for 'type'

Sheen – lustrous effect, brilliance of coat when in peak condition

Shoulder – that portion of the body from the neck back through the 5th rib and the upper joint of the foreleg.

Silvering – the mixture in the coat of white tipped guard hairs, as desired in Silvers and Meissener Lops, but even a little silvering is a fault in non-silvered breeds

Sire – father

Slate – the bottom colour in Agouti and Chinchilla, Black, Blue and Brown

The silver coat of a Silver Grey.

Smellers – whiskers

Smut – darker nose markings

Snipey – narrow elongated head

Sore Hock – ulceration above the footpad. Caused on the back hocks by thin bedding or stamping.

Speck Eye – small white specks in the iris of the eye

Sperms – the reproductive cells produced by the buck

Standard – the Breed Standard allocates a total of 100 points for the judge to award to the various attributes required for the breed. Breed Clubs submit a 'Standard' to the BRC for scrutiny and approval before it is accepted for the official Breed Standards Book.

Stockings – the dark markings on the legs of Himalayans

Stops – white markings on the hind feet of Dutch rabbits to cut cleanly into leg colour

Strain – a genetically related bloodline possessing distinguishing characteristics such as type, colour or coat, and the ability to pass the characteristic on to the offspring

Stud – a collection of rabbits where breeding usually takes place

Stud Buck – a buck used for mating, usually no longer used for showing

T

Tan Pattern – the pattern found in Tans, Fox and Martens

Tear Drops – a fault found in English in the shape of small coloured spots below the eye

Texture – the quality of the fur – generally the silkier the coat the better in the fur and rex varieties

Ticking – hairs of a different colour to the main coat, can be desirable in Tan pattern rabbits or unwanted in selfs

Tipping – the guard hairs

Tortoiseshell (Tort) – an alternative term for the colour Madagascar or Sooty Fawn. A sandy yellow colour with black shadings.

Triangle – a small area behind the ears, which is generally lighter in colour than the rest of the coat. A feature of Tan and Agouti patterned rabbits.

Trimming – the illegal removal of hairs etc, to improve the look of an exhibit

Tufts – the ear furnishings of an Angora

Ticking is desirable in this Chocolate Silver Fox.

Type – the appearance and conformation of the rabbit

U

Undercolour – the colour at the base of the fur shaft or next to the skin

Undercut – the line of demarcation on the belly between the white saddle and the hindquarters of the Dutch

The Swiss Fox is one breed that must not have a woolly coat.

V

Variety – a distinct breed such as Havana, Angora, Mini Lop as opposed to various colours within a breed

Vent Disease – a venereal disease in rabbits that affects both sexes and is highly contagious

VHD – Viral Haemorrhagic Disease. Fatal in rabbits, can successfully be vaccinated against.

W

Wall-eye – an eye that is whitish on the surface (cornea), having a milky film over the eye. Often appears in one eye only thus giving the rabbit the appearance of having different coloured eyes. A serious fault in show rabbits.

Weaning – the removal of youngsters from their dam

White Toenail – a nail without pigmentation, showing only pink cast in the blood vessel

Wooliness – a type of fur showing the character of wool rather than fur, a fault in the Cashmere and Swiss Fox coats

Wry Neck – carriage of the head to one side at an angular plane, instead of the normal carriage in the vertical plane, often caused by a deep-seated middle ear infection

7 • Health, Hygiene and Common Rabbit Diseases

Rabbits are naturally healthy animals; a well-fed, well-housed and well-loved rabbit will generally speaking be a happy and vigorous companion. The observant rabbit keeper will spot the slightest downturn in a rabbit's demeanour and quickly take action to prevent the situation escalating.

Check your rabbit's eye – is it bright and alert?

10 Big Questions to Ask Yourself Every Time You Feed Your Rabbit

Daily Health Check

1 Is the hutch secure – no signs of attempted break-in?
2 Is bedding dry? – a damp rabbit is not a happy one.
3 Does your rabbit come forward to greet you – if not why not?
4 Has your rabbit eaten all of its previous meal – if not why not?
5 Has water been drunk from the bottle? – check bottle is working first.
6 Is water bottle completely empty? – check bottle is not broken
7 Check droppings in the hutch –is there any sign or smell of diarrhoea?
8 Check your rabbit's eye – is it bright and alert?
9 Check the rabbit's mouth is clean and dry – no slobbers or dribbles?
10 Check inside of rabbit's front legs – no matting or signs of nasal discharge?

Rabbits thrive on routine in their lives; they should be fed at the same time every day, the main parts of their meals, pellets/mix, hay and water should be the same every day and delivered in the same way. If you keep to rigid routines with your rabbit then you will quickly notice if anything is wrong. If there is no routine

Pride in your rabbit

Children love to be with their rabbits but remember to wash after contact with a rabbit.

Hygiene Rules

1 Wash your hands after handling a rabbit or cleaning out a hutch.
2 Wash the rabbit's food bowls and water bottles separately from the household's washing-up. Keep a separate washing-up bowl for washing the rabbit's bowl and bottle. Do not drain washed-up rabbit bowls and bottles on the kitchen drainer. Dry the rabbit's bowl and bottle with a tea towel kept especially for it or with paper towels.
3 Store rabbit food separately from your own and keep it in sealable containers to prevent access by vermin. Buy dry food in small quantities only, so that it is fresh when fed to your rabbit.
4 Never bring rabbits into or near the place where your food is stored or prepared.
5 Never eat, drink or smoke while playing with your rabbit or while cleaning out the hutch. Be careful to avoid doing anything that may transfer dirt from the rabbit or hutch to your lips.
6 When young children play with a rabbit or clean a hutch, an adult should supervise to ensure that children follow these rules and that they learn the elements of good hygiene.

then it is hard to spot anything out of the ordinary. *Carry out the Daily Health Check* every time you feed your rabbit.

If you keep more than one rabbit then you should have somewhere prepared so that you can immediately isolate any rabbit that you suspect of being sick. This should be a warm, well-ventilated location away from harsh lighting. Many of the common rabbit ailments are highly contagious; rapid isolation can prevent a disease spreading to other animals. Many of the rabbit diseases can prove fatal if not treated promptly; the severity of the signs should dictate your next course of action. If the signs are minor, or rather vague, you might wait for 12–24 hours to see if things return to normal. If they do not then a Veterinarian should be contacted as soon as possible after you have confirmed the problem as they are the trained experts in small animal care. Do not leave it until later by which time a simple problem may have escalated to a far more serious one. Rabbits are not good patients; rather than fight an illness, many seem to give up as soon as they feel ill. Quick action is called for.

Some rabbit diseases can be transmitted to humans (they are shown in italics), particularly children. The Hygiene Rules, facing page, should prevent this happening:

Clean, secure hutches mean happy, healthy rabbits

Diseases

Abscesses (*see also* Tapeworm Cyst) – can occur anywhere as a result of cuts or wounds. Should heal if treated promptly by a veterinarian.

Anaemia/Listlessness – anaemia is easily detected in albino breeds when the red of the eye is dull or even pink. Give plenty of green foods especially those rich in iron, e.g. parsley.

Bloat (Blows) – common condition in half-grown youngsters, the stomach becomes distended and full of gas. Very distressing for the rabbit. The rabbit may be saved by prompt action, seek veterinary advice immediately.

Bald Patches – *see* Mange (below). Rabbits are born bald and do not start to fur-up until about 10 days old.

Blindness – rabbits are born blind, their eyes open at about 10 days.

Canker – caused by very small mites who get into the inner surface of the ear and cause irritation to it; there is a thin discharge from the ear that hardens and forms a crust. The rabbit shakes its head and scratches its ear. The infected ear has a distinctive smell. Can be treated with eardrops from a veterinarian.

Cannibalism – Does (female rabbits) sometimes eat their young at time of birth. Thought to be due to thirst; give the doe a large bowl of fresh water at time of kindling.

Coccidiosis – Young rabbits fail to gain weight, sit hunched-up in the corner with their back legs extended forward, in bad cases there is severe diarrhoea with rapid weight loss and the rabbit has a pot-bellied look. Microscopic parasites infest either the liver or the lining of the intestine. Caused by poor husbandry, young rabbit eating fouled food or drinking water infected with the oocysts or eggs. Many rabbit feeds now have an additive that prevents Coccidiosis. Seek veterinary advice immediately.

Conjunctivitis – Inflammation of the eye – common in bucks especially during heavy moult. Eye drops from a veterinarian should clear the problem.

Constipation – the passing of only a few very dried up pellets – increase green foods to cure.

Convulsions – caused by over-mating of either buck or doe, overcrowded conditions as youngsters grow, general poor, unhealthy conditions in rabbitry. Isolate any rabbits suffering and radically improve the living conditions in which they are kept; survival a possibility, but future uses for breeding unlikely.

Coprophagy (or reingestion) – you may see your rabbit eat its own droppings. This is quite natural. Rabbits have to eat their food twice, and your rabbit is re-ingesting half eaten food. The half-digested pellet is black, sticky and smelly. If you find a lot of these pellets uneaten in the hutch something is disturbing the rabbit from its natural task – is there a dog or cat threatening your rabbit?

Cuts and Wounds – add a drop of mild disinfectant to some boiled and cooled water, and bathe the wound gently. If it does not heal within a couple of days seek veterinary advice.

Cyst – there are two types of worm cysts in rabbits. One is found in the liver and the other under the skin. They are caused by rabbits eating green food that has been fouled by dogs. The liver cyst often proves fatal, the ones under the skin do little damage and can be removed by a veterinarian.

Dandruff – usually appears as fine greyish-white scales on the skin and fur behind the neck where the rabbit may scratch it. Usually appears on rabbits kept in small hutches in hot weather. Improving living conditions, exercise and diet will cure it.

Diarrhoea (Scours) – may be the symptom of something more serious. Discontinue green food and give hay only. Astringents such as shepherd's purse, strawberry or raspberry leaves will help. If not cured in 24 hours seek veterinary advice.

Ear Canker – *see* Canker

Ear Mites – *see* Canker

Electric Shock – if your rabbit has bitten through an electric cable and is laying either unconscious or semi-conscious: turn off power before touching the rabbit then cover with blanket and keep warm whilst you call a veterinarian.

Eyes – if eyes become damaged or eyelids torn, consult a veterinarian. Eyes may become inflamed for a number of reasons: draughts, dust, bucks spraying urine, fumes from urine in hutch. A veterinarian will prescribe eye drops.

Fleas – like all animals with fur coats rabbits can get fleas; they are usually seen first where the fur is thinnest around ears or on belly. Black specks of flea droppings will probably be seen before the actual fleas. The rabbit flea is one of the vectors that carry Myxomatosis. Flea treatment from a veterinarian will get rid of them.

Fly Strike – fly strike is perhaps the most disgusting thing you will ever see and it is entirely preventable with good animal husbandry. A fly attracted by the smell of diarrhoea lays its eggs in the faeces–soiled fur. Within 24 hours the maggots hatch and burrow into the rabbits flesh where they literally eat the rabbit's soft tissue. By the time you discover it, the flesh will be heaving with maggots; the agony this causes the rabbit cannot be imagined. Rabbits discovered to have fly strike should be taken to the vet immediately and possibly put down.

Heat Stroke/Exhaustion – in very hot weather, rabbits enclosed in a hutch are liable to heat stroke. Signs – panting, gasping for air, listlessness, lays on back trying to cool stomach. Prevention is better than cure. Move hutch to cooler spot, run water over hutch, hang wet towel over door area (will need frequently replacing as it dries), frozen bottles of water can be placed in hutch, a cool ceramic tile for rabbit to lay on. Cure – remove rabbit to cool place, lay a wet towel over rabbit or mist with cool water, give 'bowl' of cool water to drink from, the stress of rushing to the vet may do more harm than good unless first aid treatments are having no effect.

Hernia – a rupture or protrusion of the abdomen contents outside the abdomen. Seek veterinary advice.

Ingrown Eyelash – can be very painful for the rabbit, seek veterinary advice

Lice – *Unlike fleas, lice lay their eggs, known as 'nits' in the fur of the host animal. The eggs are white and attach themselves to the hair shaft. They show up well on dark-coloured rabbits and will be seen as white specks in the coat when grooming. Seek veterinary advice for treatment. Can be transmitted to humans.*

Listeriosis – *disease, resembling influenza,*

caused by infection with a type of bacterium (listeria) from contaminated food, may cause miscarriages in does. Contagious to humans.

Mange – *a parasitic complaint that is caused by small mites burrowing under the skin resulting in scabs that appear first on the head and then on the legs, feet and body. The fur drops out and the rabbit scratches continually. Seek veterinary advice – contagious to humans.*

Megrims, Dizziness, Fits – nervous disorder, the rabbit may carry its head on one side or swing it from side to side. Usually attributed to a defect in the digestive organs, which affect the nerves. In extreme cases the rabbit 'fits'. Careful attention to diet, addition of dandelion and clover, may help. Otherwise seek veterinary advice.

Mites – several different mites affect rabbits. The ear mite (*see above*) causes ear canker whilst the forage or harvest mite burrow into the skin and causes intense irritation which the rabbit will scratch until it is raw; this condition is also known as Mange (*see above*).

Mucoid Enteritis – also known as bloat, scours or diarrhoea. This infection accounts for a very high percentage of deaths in young rabbits although can affect rabbits of all ages. Rabbits appear listless, lose their appetite, have dull squinting eyes, gritting and grinding of teeth, thirst, sloshing of stomach contents. The youngster may be constipated or may have diarrhoea and pass a clear jelly- like substance. Seek veterinary advice – prognosis is not good.

Myxomatosis – deadly viral disease; transmitted from the wild rabbit population by the rabbit flea or mosquitoes. Clinical signs include swelling of the eyelids until the rabbit is unable to open its eyes, and swelling of the nose, mouth and anus. Vaccinate regularly for immunisation. Infected rabbits rarely recover.

Paralysis – usually attacks the hind quarters, caused by being dropped, mishandled, or attacked by rats, dogs, foxes etc. Keep warm and quiet for up to two weeks – may recover. Seek veterinary advice.

Pneumonia – acute disease, rabbit holds its head high and tilted backwards, breathes with difficulty and has a mucus discharge from mouth, nasal passages and eyes; prompt veterinary attention *may* save the rabbit. Usually caused by poor animal husbandry. Seek veterinary advice.

Pseudo-tuberculosis – *infected rabbits rapidly lose weight and develop diarrhoea. The infection is caught by eating greens soiled by wild birds and other rabbits. It spreads to humans when hands become contaminated with diarrhoea and hygiene is inadequate. Seek veterinary advice.*

Obesity – Too much food, too little exercise

will kill the rabbit. More exercise and less food may save a severely overweight rabbit, but heart failure is highly likely.

Ophthalmia – swollen or closed eyes. Common, especially in young rabbits kept in poor conditions. Improve living conditions, especially ventilation. Bathe eyes with warm saline solution, if no improvement, seek veterinary advice.

Overgrown Claws – clipping rabbit claws is not difficult and as they will require doing frequently for hutch-kept rabbits it is best to get an experienced rabbit keeper or veterinarian expert to teach you how to do it (*see feature on page 80*).

Overgrown Teeth – overgrown teeth are usually a result of bad breeding. A vet can trim the teeth before they get long enough to cause the rabbit discomfort (probably as often as once a month), check teeth when buying your rabbit and do not buy one with maloccluded teeth (*see feature on page 82*)

Pot-Belly – common condition in half grown youngsters, the stomach becomes distended and full of gas. Very distressing for the rabbit. The rabbit may be saved by prompt action, seek veterinary advice immediately.

Red Water – Due to cold and damp affecting kidneys. Too many diuretic greens i.e. dandelions may show same symptoms, as will

Healthy Mother and Son enjoy a treat

beetroot. Ensure rabbit has warm, dry bedding and reduce or withhold green food for a couple of days. If no better, seek veterinary advice.

Rickets – Very weak in legs; common in badly-kept rabbitries lacking light, sunshine and a diet deficient in vitamins A and D. Improve husbandry and seek veterinary advice.

Ring Worm *– a fungal disease that causes* *circular bald patches on the head and feet. It is especially infectious to children who cuddle their pet rabbit. Seek veterinary advice. Contagious to humans.*

Salmonellosis *– bacterium associated with food poisoning in man. Infected rabbits will have diarrhoea, pregnant does may abort litters. Seek veterinary advice. Contagious to humans.*

Sexual Inflammation – *see* Vent Disease

Slobbers or Acute Indigestion – usually caused by infected teeth or abscesses. The rabbit drools and wipes its mouth with front legs. Difficult to cure. Seek veterinary advice.

Snuffles (Sneezing) and Colds – infection of the respiratory tract, correctly known as 'contagious rhinitis', characterised by a thick, yellowish discharge from nose, continual sneezing, inside of front legs will become matted where rabbit has wiped its nose with legs. May develop into pneumonia if not treated quickly – isolate immediately, highly contagious – very difficult to cure. Seek veterinary advice.

Sore Hocks – thin fur on hocks may be an inherited defect. Nervous or stressed rabbits that do a lot of stamping are prone to it, especially if bedding is thin. Seek veterinary advice.

Stoppage of the Bowels – *see* Constipation

Swollen Teats/Mastitis – congestion of the milk glands, may occur when a doe loses her litter or has litter of only one. Mammary glands become hot, hard and painful. Bathing with a warm cloth may help. Otherwise seek veterinary advice.

Tapeworm Cyst – a lump that can appear anywhere on the body and may grow as large as an egg. Usually caused by rabbit eating green food that has been fouled by a dog. Seek veterinary advice – expect full recovery.

Tick – a parasite that attaches itself to a rabbit, feeding on the rabbit's blood for several days until sufficiently bloated to drop off naturally. NOTE: can only be picked up by the rabbit running free in garden or by contact with contaminated hay or straw. If this is the case change your supplier.

Tuberculosis – airborne virus, check ventilation in rabbitry. Breathing sounds harsh; rabbit may eat ravenously but lose weight – isolate immediately. Seek veterinary advice.

Vent Disease (Hutch Burn) – Rabbit syphilis, scabs or sores on reproductive organs. If rabbit licks infected reproductive organs scabs will appear on face as well. Highly contagious at mating. Seek veterinary advice.

VHD – Viral Haemorrhagic Disease – fatal – vaccinate regularly to immunise.

Worms – small round worms are very occasionally found in the droppings. Seek veterinary advice.

Wry Neck – rabbit holds head to one side, may be as bad as to lose balance, caused by deep-seated ear infection. Seek veterinary advice.

Cutting Rabbit Nails

Just like our nails, rabbit's nails grow continually and just as we do not wear our toenails down naturally neither does a rabbit that is kept on soft bedding in a hutch. A hutch-kept rabbit will need its nails cut at least twice a year as overgrown nails start by becoming uncomfortable but soon become painful. A rabbit that regularly runs free in the house or garden may need them cutting less frequently. Make a nail check part of your weekly health check (*see page 88*)

If you are unsure of how to hold the rabbit and how to cut the nails it is best to get either an experienced rabbit fancier or a veterinarian to teach you. The cutting of very large rabbit's nails is not for the faint-hearted as they may struggle and kick out; it is easier if two people work together to cut a large and uncooperative rabbit's nails.

Extra care is required when cutting black nails.

When to cut the nails

The cut nail should be about a ¼ inch (6mm) longer than the quick, which can clearly be seen through the nail. When nails are ½ – ¾ inch (12mm – 19mm) long they should be cut. Do not forget the dewclaw on the inside of the front legs.

How to cut nails

In good natural day light sit on a low chair or stool so that the top of your legs form a flat base to lay the rabbit on. Lay the rabbit on its back between your legs with its head furthest away from you and get it settled and calm. Rabbits will soon settle in this position if they feel secure.

Hold the nail clippers in one hand, your cutting hand, and one of the rabbit's feet in the other. Use your forefinger and thumb to hold the toe of the nail you wish to cut. Cut with your nail clippers 'fore and aft', not sideways across the nail; make the cut about ¼ inch (6mm) above the quick. The quick is easily seen on rabbits with light coloured nails but more difficult to see on dark-nailed rabbits. Do all the nails on one foot before moving on to the next foot so that nails do not get missed.

Holding your rabbit confidently makes the job so much easier.

TIP: The best nail clippers to use

Pet shops sell small dog nail clippers that are ideal for rabbit's nails.

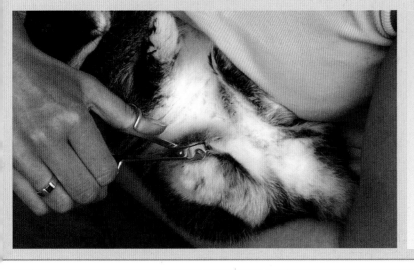

TIP: First aid

Pet shops and vets sell a powder (Trimex is one such product) that can be applied to stop bleeding should you accidentally cut the quick. It is always worth having such a product handy before you start trimming your rabbit's nails.

Rabbit Teeth

The front or incisor teeth of rabbits grow continually throughout their lives. Wild rabbits keep them short by continually gnawing at branches, bark, roots and other hard foods. If you feed your rabbit on a proprietary brand of rabbit food (mix or pellets) then it should have sufficient hard material in it to wear the rabbit's teeth as it grinds the food down. If your rabbit lacks sufficient gnawing material, its incisor teeth may grow longer and longer until in some cases the rabbit cannot eat. In this case your rabbit should be encouraged to chew by giving plenty of fresh hay or chewing material such as cabbage, cauliflower or Brussels sprout stalks, or a gnawing block. Pet shops now sell a whole range of gnawing products for rabbits.

In some rabbits, the teeth are positioned incorrectly in the mouth so that they do not work against each other and wear down properly. This is an inherited trait known as 'malocclusion'. Rabbits suffering from malocclusion should not be used in a breeding programme and cannot be shown in rabbit shows. Maloccluded rabbits will need to have their teeth clipped by a veterinarian on a regular basis

Incorrectly aligned teeth can cause problems.

Class III Malocclusion – the lower teeth stick out past the upper teeth, this is also called an 'underbite'.

Class II Malocclusion – the upper teeth stick out past the lower, this is called an 'overbite' or buck teeth. Rabbits should have a slight overbite, but not an excessive one.

Class I Malocclusion – the bite is OK (the top teeth line up with the bottom teeth) but your teeth are crooked, crowded or turned.

TIP: Make your own gnawing block

You can make your own gnawing block from a freshly cut branch, apple is their favorite, leave the bark on – they love tearing it off and chewing it.

TOP
A perfect set of teeth

LEFT
Maloccluded teeth

83

8 • *Rabbit Routines*

Animal husbandry, or to be more specific, rabbit husbandry is all about setting up regular routines and sticking to them. In the wild a rabbit's routines are laid down annually, seasonally and even daily, usually being dictated by the weather. Anything that upsets those routines is likely to bring chaos to the rabbit's life – those who have read Richard Adams's wonderful book, *Watership Down*, will appreciate just how the lives of the main characters were turned upside down by man.

Most of us lead a fairly orderly life and it really should not be too difficult to fit your rabbit's routines into your everyday lifestyle. Try to establish the following routines for your rabbit:

Your rabbit relies on you to set up routines for feeding and cleaning.

1 Daily Life-Pattern Routine
2 Daily Feeding Routine
3 Daily Health Check
4 Daily Cleaning Routine
5 Weekly Cleaning Routine
6 Weekly Health Check
7 Weekly Grooming Routine
8 Bi-annual Cleaning Routine
9 Bi-annual Health Check
10 Seasonal Life Pattern Routine

1. Daily Life-Pattern Routine

Hutch rabbits like to sleep during the hours of darkness in the summer. They also like to sleep during the afternoon in both the summer and winter. Therefore you should:

➤ 'Open Up' and say 'good morning' to your rabbit fairly early in the morning and carry out your
  • Daily Health Check
  • Feed and Water
  • Carry out Daily Cleaning

➤ Play time, human contact time or put out in 'run' in the cool of the morning

➤ Afternoon in hutch left in peace to sleep
  • Early evening contact/training/grooming time followed by the evening feed

➤ 'Close Up' and say 'Good night'. Have a final security check either at last light or just before you go to bed in the summer.

2. Daily Feeding Routine

⮞ Morning
- Clean out any left over food, greens or hay trodden into the floor
- Check and replenish hay
- Wash and refill water bottle
- Give half daily ration of pellets or rabbit mix
- Mix of fresh greens

⮞ Evening
- Check water bottle and refill if necessary
- Give other half daily ration of pellets or rabbit mix

3. Daily Health Check

Your daily health check will become, with practice, a very quick check over your rabbit to make sure all is well; it should include a look at the following:

⮞ Does your rabbit come to greet you at the front of the hutch – if not why not?

⮞ Has last night's food been eaten – if not why not?

⮞ Has some water been drunk, if not why not? – check bottle is working properly

⮞ Look into your rabbit's eyes, they should be clear and bright

Your rabbit should be bright-eyed.

⮞ Look at your rabbit's nose it should be clear and dry

⮞ Look at your rabbit's mouth – it should be clear and dry

⮞ Run your hand over your rabbit's back as if stroking it, check for lumps, cuts or scratches

85

Human contact time.

➤ Check with your hand, nose, and eyes around the back end of your rabbit. Take immediate action if the coat is soiled with diarrhoea.

4. Daily Cleaning Routine

➤ Clean food bowl

➤ Clean water bottle (*see page 33*)

➤ Clean out any left-over food or hay that has fallen to the floor.

➤ Clean out the 'dirty corner' or litter tray if you have managed to litter train.

Your rabbit's nose should be dry and clean.

Give half the daily ration of pellets.

5. Weekly Cleaning Routine

All rabbit hutches should be cleaned out completely at least once a week; in hot weather or for a particularly dirty rabbit it should be more often.

- Remove rabbit to a safe location, either in a run or 'boxed'.

- Remove all food bowls, toys and gnawing blocks.

- Using a dustpan and brush, kept especially for the job, clear out all the straw and shavings from the hutch. This fouled bedding does make excellent compost for the garden if you have the space to create a compost heap, though it does take rather a long time to rot down (about a year).

- Scrub out the inside of the hutch using a pet disinfectant, rinse well with clean water.

- Allow to dry

- Put a good deep layer (about 1" (25mm) deep) of 'pet wood shavings' on the entire floor of the hutch and sleeping compartment.
  - **Do not** put a layer of newspaper under the shaving; rabbits chew the newspaper, it can form a ball in the gut and as it is indigestible it may block the stomach with serious consequences.
  - **Do not** use sawdust as a replacement for wood shavings, the dust gets in the rabbit's eyes and then it will be a trip to the veterinarian to cure its irritated eyes.

- Add a layer of soft, clean Barley Straw; extra straw in the depths of winter will keep your rabbit warm.

- Return clean bowls, bottle, chews and toys to hutch.

- Return rabbit to hutch.

6. Weekly Health Check

Every week when you carry out your *Weekly Cleaning* you should carry out a *Weekly Health Check* on your rabbit. This includes your *Daily Health Check* but is a lot more thorough and should identify a problem before it gets serious and causes the rabbit discomfort. At first sight it may seem that you have a lot to do but with a little practice you will find that it actually only takes a couple of minutes and it will be a couple of minutes well spent.

Start at the front of the rabbit and work towards the back end, checking all of the following:

- **Nose** – should be clear and dry with no discharge.

- **Teeth** – should be clean and white, the top teeth should just overlap the bottom ones.

Make a check to ensure they have not been damaged or have anything stuck in them.

Eyes – should be clear and bright with no discharge of any kind.

Ears – run your fingers over both ears and check for damage to the ears; especially look for nicks or cuts and clean and treat if

necessary. Look in and 'smell' the inside of the ears they should be clean and free from any waxing or sign of disease.

Turn the rabbit over on its back

Front and Back legs – and look at the front feet, they should be clean, run your fingers along the legs and feet, check for

Add a layer of soft Barley Straw to the clean hutch as it provides both warmth and food for your rabbit.

any damage. Check the pads of each foot they should be well furred. Check the inside of the front legs for any matting, rabbits use the inside of their front legs to wipe their noses, so any matting may indicate some nasal discharge.

Nails – Check the nails. If they need cutting, do them now, do not put it off.

Genitals – they should be clean and free from any signs of disease. This is probably

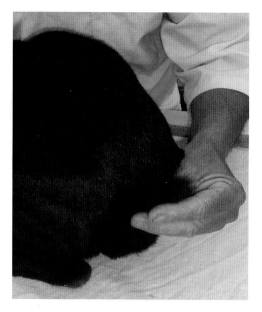

Run your fingers up the length of the tail and check for irregularities.

the first place you will see signs of general ill health.

Sit the rabbit back on its feet

Run your hands over its back – with your fingers feel along the ribs and up into the groin, there should be no lumps or irregularities. Check the coat for bald patches or any infestation, rabbit fleas are not uncommon and can usually be seen in the very thin fur around the ears or on the belly.

Tail – run your fingers up the length of the tail and check for any irregularities; it should be straight with no kinks or breaks in it

7. Weekly Grooming Routine

The amount of grooming that is required each week will vary throughout the year as much more work will be required when your rabbit is moulting than during the rest of the year. You can carry out your Weekly Grooming at the same time as your other weekly tasks (Weekly Health Check and Weekly Cleaning).

Normal Coat (when your rabbit is not moulting):
- Sit your rabbit on a non-slip grooming table – this can be a small piece of carpet (carpet samples are ideal – free from a carpet shop) placed on a table or

Weekly grooming keeps your rabbit in good condition.

bench at a suitable height for you to work at.

- Dampen you hands (rub them with a damp cloth) and then work them from the back end of the rabbit towards its head so that you make the rabbit's coat stand up on end; it will soon return to its normal position. Do this a few times – it will bring out the dead hairs and any dust that the coat has picked up from the wood shavings and straw. You can use a soft dog grooming brush over the coat but your dampened hands will do a much better job.
- Use a fine comb (dog grooming ones are best) to very gently comb around the rump of the rabbit. Check the underneath around the genitals; this area may need combing – do so with *extreme care*.
- Sit the rabbit back on all fours and use a piece of velvet or soft chamois to rub the coat over, working from head to tail this time, and bring out that lovely healthy shine.

Coat in Moult

- The moult is a natural phenomenon where the rabbit replaces its thick winter coat with a new thinner summer coat. It normally takes place during the summer months, but rabbits kept sheltered from the elements can moult at almost any time. It is quite amazing how much hair comes out of a rabbit during its moult, which may last for many weeks.

- You can assist your rabbit through the moult by regular grooming.
- Pet Shops sell what are known as 'rubber scrubbers' for grooming cats and dogs; the dog version is a bit hard and heavy for rabbits but the cat version is absolutely perfect for shifting a moulty coat. Use the rubber scrubber by brushing in the direction of the coat i.e. from head to tail.
- You can further aid the moult by careful use of comb – be very careful with the comb as a rabbit's skin is quite thin and tears very easily.

8. Bi-annual Cleaning Routine

The big bi-annual clean really is a complete overhaul of the hutch in the spring to check for damage incurred over the winter and any infestation of microorganisms and again in the autumn to prepare for the winter. In April and October carry out the following:

➤ Place the rabbit somewhere safe for the next 24 hours.

➤ Completely empty the hutch.

➤ Check over bowl, bottle, hayrack, toys and chews – do any need replacing?

➤ Check over hutch paying particular attention to;
- Security – check all catches and doors
- Check roofing for water-proofness.
- Check wire netting on door – replace any damaged wire.
- Check inside of hutch for damage from either chewing or damp seepage/rot – make good any damage.

➤ Thoroughly scrub inside of hutch with pet-safe disinfectant

➤ Using appropriate safety precautions use a blow-torch to scorch the inside of the hutch, paying particular attention to all joints and cracks – this will kills off any microorganisms that the disinfectant has missed.

➤ When the hutch is thoroughly dry, paint the internal floor with waterproof pet safe bitumen paint.

➤ Allow the hutch to dry overnight so that floor is completely dry before putting new bedding and either new or cleaned equipment back in the hutch.

➤ Put the rabbit back in the hutch and feed it.

9. Bi-annual Health Check

Take your rabbit to the veterinarian twice a year for a full check up and to have booster vaccinations for Myxomatosis and VHD. Both these diseases are killers of rabbits and yet are completely avoidable if vaccinations are kept up to date.

air in the summer so we must make a similar adjustment to how we keep our rabbit, ensuring that it is comfortable and healthy throughout the year. See the section on 'Caring for your Rabbit through the Seasons'.

10. Seasonal Life Pattern Routine

Just as we close the doors and windows to keep out the cold and wet during the winter yet throw them wide open for the warmth and fresh

Healthy rabbits are happy rabbits.

9 • *Showing Your Rabbit*

The proud winner of Best Pet Rabbit at a pet show run alongside a BRC Show.

Showing Your Rabbit

Part of the fun of owning a rabbit is taking it to pet or rabbit shows and competing against others people's rabbits. Of course some people are very competitive and go to shows to win and anything less is a disappointment to them, whilst other people go for the day out, to be with and talk to people with a kindred interest in rabbits.

There are two types of show where you can exhibit your rabbit, the local pet show and the British Rabbit Council supported show, and they are very different.

Local Pet Shows

At local pet shows the judge, who may not be a rabbit specialist, will be assessing all the pets presented to them for three qualities;

◄ condition,
◄ cleanliness
◄ friendliness

Now this can be extremely difficult for the judge, who may well have to assess rabbits, hamsters, rats, budgies, stick insects and goldfish, in fact any pet that you can think of all in the same class. Nevertheless a good rabbit in cracking condition that is immaculately clean and shows a bit of character and friendliness towards the judge stands just as good a chance as any of the other animals.

Your rabbit does not need to be a pedigree, although it can be, it does not have to conform to any breed standard or colour pattern. In fact it is often the mis-marked rabbits that catch the judge's eye and one ear up and one down often has an appeal for him as long as the rabbit is clean and in good condition.

Exhibiting at these shows does require you to train your rabbit (*see* Training Your Rabbit page 100) and any prize that you win will reflect how well you have done so.

Generally they are a grand day out,

Children's pet show

especially for children, and preparing the rabbit for the show is a great way of teaching children pet responsibility.

Many of the BRC Supported rabbit shows hold a pet show alongside the main event. These pet shows are open to anyone and are

run on the same lines as the local pet show described above. Because they are held in the same hall and alongside the main show they are a great window on what really happens at the BRC Supported Shows. Here you will meet and be able to talk to rabbit fanciers, many of whom will have had a lifetime's experience in breeding, raising, keeping and showing rabbits.

British Rabbit Council Supported Shows

The British Rabbit Council (BRC) is the governing body for rabbit breeders and exhibitors in Britain. It has been in existence, in its present format, since the 1930's and its headquarters are at Purefoy House, 7 Kirkgate, Newark, Notts NG24 1AD. The BRC is administered by a full time secretarial staff but is run by a Management Committee of elected rabbit fanciers.

To exhibit rabbits at a BRC supported show you must first be a fully paid-up member of the BRC and then your rabbit must wear a BRC ring on one of its back legs. This ring is a unique identification system for each rabbit registered with the BRC, it is fitted by the breeder when the rabbit is young and stays on the rabbit's legs for life. Each breed is allocated a ring size (each size has a different letter from A–X) so the ring should stay on the rabbit and cause no problem throughout its life; many breeders cut the ring off if a rabbit is being retired from showing and sold as a pet.

Within the structure of the BRC there is a

Products are available to prepare your rabbit for the pet show. Nail trimmers, brush and shampoo could all help you get a prize.

The spoils of victory

Breed Standards Committee whose responsibility it is to administer the Breed Standard put forward by Breed Specialist Club for each breed. The Breed Standard awards 100 points for the desired characteristics and traits of a breed, it is this Breed Standard that all rabbits are judged against at BRC supported shows. All rabbits exhibited under BRC rules must be pedigrees (true-bred) and must conform as closely as possible to the Standard required for its breed as well as a list of general requirements relating to health and condition. This may all sound somewhat daunting but the *Oxford Dictionary* definition of 'Fancier' may explain just why 'the art or practice of breeding animals so as to develop particular points'. So you can see that rabbit fanciers are continually striving to breed rabbits that more closely resemble the required Breed Standard than anyone else's.

The BRC has an official magazine called *The Fur and Feather* which can be bought through their office at Elder House, Chattisham, Ipswich, Suffolk IP8 3QE. *Fur and Feather* also have an extensive bookshop selling specialist rabbit books, but it is their monthly magazine that is an absolute must for all rabbit fanciers. As well as wealth of useful information and news about rabbits *The Fur and Feather* lists all the upcoming shows and entry details together

with the results and judges comments on the winners of past shows.

Both the BRC and *The Fur and Feather* can be contacted through their official websites www.thebrc.org and www.furandfeather.co.uk

Anyone interested in taking up the 'rabbit habit' and becoming a fancier would be advised to visit a couple of BRC supported rabbit shows first to see what they are like and if it really is for them. All upcoming shows are listed on the BRC website. A short book entitled *Showing Rabbits* by Geoff Russell (ISBN 1-898015-07-4) is available from *The Fur and Feather* bookshop and is an excellent easy guide to introduce the newcomer to the world of showing rabbits.

LEFT The London Championship Show – a successful days showing.

Judging at a local BRC supported show.

10 • *Training Your Rabbit*

What do you want your rabbit to be?

⤷ House rabbit pet/companion

⤷ Hutch/Garden Pet

⤷ Pet plus Local Pet/Rabbit Shows

⤷ BRC Supported Show rabbit

The training your rabbit needs to meet the requirements of each of these roles is slightly different though there is one basic requirement no matter what you intend to do with your rabbit – it must learn to be sociable and easy to handle, although even the level of sociability will vary with the rabbit's role. You do not want a show rabbit climbing up the judge's shoulder for 'kisses' which may be acceptable behaviour for a pet, but most certainly is not on the show bench.

Training a House Rabbit Pet/Companion

⤷ Socialising – start handling early, 'little and often' is the answer as young rabbits, like young children, tire quickly. Do not overwhelm the young rabbit; if you sit on the floor the rabbit's natural inquisitiveness will bring it to you where you can stroke it and allow it to climb onto you. It will soon learn to associate you with kindness and the caring attention that all rabbits seek.

Even a house rabbit should have a secure bed area that it can be shut into for safety whilst you are sleeping or are out of the house. They learn from a very young age that this is 'their safe area', their bed. You are certainly not doing them any favours leaving them out in a hostile environment while you are not there to supervise them.

Start socialising early – little and often.

Sharing the garden

A commercial brand of rabbit chew that will help your rabbit to exercise its natural desire to chew discouraging damaging objects in the home.

- Start litter training early in the rabbit's life – it comes quite naturally to most rabbits and will make your life easier and your house cleaner the quicker it learns. Do not shout at or hit a rabbit, this will not help to train them but will just scare them. Kindness and patience are what work.

- Fact – rabbits chew!!

- Protect your wires, behind the TV; telephone, etc, in plastic tubing.

- If a rabbit chews furniture or wall paper spray 'Bitter Apple' or a similar product so that it tastes bitter to the rabbit and it learns not to chew – again shouting or hitting do not work.

- If you find your rabbit attacks one particular member of the family it is usually 'scent related'. It may be a perfume, a particular soap or hand cream or even an aftershave that it has taken a dislike to. Some trial and error work should soon isolate what it is that rabbit does not like and harmony can be restored in the household.

- It is worth taking a young rabbit for a few short trips in the car, in a secure, well-ventilated box. This teaches them that they will come home again and then when they do have to go in the car, to the vets or on holiday it is far less stressful for them.

TIP: How to pick your rabbit up

1 Have the rabbit facing you on a firm surface. Grasp the ears firmly with one hand, the other hand cupping the rump.

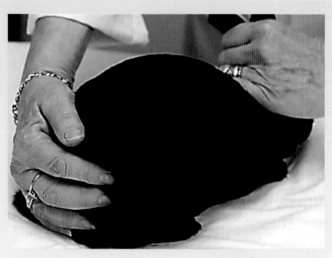

2 Lift from the back so the rabbit's weight is supported in one palm while the other hand steadies the head by holding the ears.

3 Clasp the rabbit to your chest supporting the weight with one hand and placing the other hand on its back. The rabbit will feel secure in this position.

Training a Hutch/Garden Pet

You may think that a rabbit that lives in a hutch in the garden needs little or no training, but perhaps the socialising of a garden kept rabbit is more important than that of a house rabbit. The hutch rabbit will not have as much contact with you and the rest of the family as one living in the house would have but you do not want to be attacked when you go near the hutch.

- Socialising – must start early, little and often, remember rabbits like to sleep in the afternoon so try and hold your training session either in the early morning or in the evening.

- Get your young rabbit used to being picked up and held every time you come to the hutch.

- Give them plenty of toys, gnawing blocks and general distracters to stop them becoming bored and frustrated during the periods they are on their own.

- Try to get them used to having a litter tray in the corner of their hutch from an early age this will make your life a lot easier in the years to come.

- It is worth taking a young hutch rabbit for a few short trips in the car, in a secure, well-ventilated box. This teaches them that they

Rabbits sleep in the afternoon.

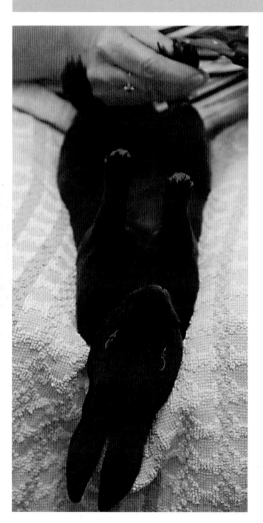

Get them used to being turned over in your lap it will make nail cutting much easier

will come home again and then when they do have to go in the car, to the vets or on holiday it is far less stressful for them.

➤ Where are you going to put rabbit when you clean out the hutch each week, you may let them have a run, you may 'box them', get them used to a cleaning routine from a young age.

➤ Get them used to being turned over in your lap from a young age this will make health checks and nail cutting much easier when they are older.

➤ It is quite natural for a doe to get grumpy when she thinks she wants mating; you do have to be careful at times like this, especially with young children – rabbit bites are really nasty and quite frightening. Use a shovel or dustpan to distract them (let them attack it) whilst you grab the food bowl. They will get over it and return to their normal loving self once the hormones have sorted themselves out.

Training a Pet for Local Pet/Rabbit Shows

Obviously your pet rabbit that you wish to show at one of your local pet shows will fall into one of the two categories above and therefore require the training described there.

At most pet shows the judge will be assessing your rabbit for three qualities;

➤ condition
➤ cleanliness
➤ friendliness

➤ There is little training you can do to ensure the **conditioning** of your rabbit other than training yourself to feed your rabbit correctly and to keep it in an airy environment that promotes a healthy coat covering a fit, muscular body.

➤ You can however, train your rabbit from a very early age to allow you to groom it; this may even include washing its feet. A judge really does expect your **rabbit to be clean**. You cannot take a dirty rabbit with stained feet and an unkempt coat and make it presentable over night.

Regular grooming should get the coat in order but perhaps the hardest part of preparing a pet rabbit for a show is getting its feet clean. Running free in the garden or on grass is out for a couple of weeks before the show. Clean bedding, that you must keep changing and keep clean is a necessity and some serious feet cleaning is in order. If you have got your rabbit used to lying on its back on your lap and having its feet handled then your task will be much easier. You can scrub (gently) your rabbit's feet using an old tooth brush and soap, dry the feet and place it in a clean hutch. If the feet are badly stained you may have to do this a few times in the couple of weeks before the show.

Show rabbits must be trained to sit in their breed's recognised 'pose'

➤ You training for **'friendliness'** should of course started at a very early age but the difference if you wish to show the rabbit is that it has to be friendly to whoever handles it and not just to you. You should therefore try to let different people turn your rabbit over and generally pet it.

★Although pet rabbits are not expected to sit in the 'pose' of a show rabbit, it does help if they will sit peacefully and at ease on the judge's table. You can train your rabbit for this by having a 'show table' at home where you can train your rabbit to sit at ease. Much of this type of training is down to the way that you handle your rabbit; if you handle it in a quiet, confident manner then the rabbit will be calm and relaxed – just how you want it for the judge's table.

Training a rabbit for British Rabbit Council (BRC) Supported Shows

To enter a BRC supported rabbit show you must be a paid-up member of the BRC and your rabbit must be wearing a 'ring' on one of its back legs that is registered in your name (see Showing Rabbits, page....). Your rabbit must be pure bred and conform to the BRC Breed Standard for the breed. If you and your rabbit meet these requirements then you will need to spend a considerable amount of time training and preparing your rabbit for the show.

★Show rabbits should be kept in hutches:
- Sunlight ruins the colour of the coat
- Gardens stain feet
- Gardens are full of dangers that can damage your rabbit

★Show rabbits must be kept in scrupulously clean conditions.

★Show rabbits must be trained to sit in the required 'pose' for the breed, this will be required for lengthy periods at some shows, and they could be on the judges table for as long as half an hour. Build a show bench at home where you can train your show rabbit from an early age. Little and often is the only way to go, do not allow rabbit to climb up on you, hold it gently in the required 'pose' and smooth it down the back with the palm of your hand. When it starts to fidget and has clearly had enough of sitting then do some grooming.

★Your show rabbit will be expected to be in perfect condition and spotlessly clean. The judge will turn it over on its back to check that it is, so get it used to being turned over and having its feet and legs touched. The judge will also check your rabbit's teeth, so again, get it used to this simple and painless procedure - if you are not sure how to do it yourself then ask an experienced fancier to show you.

The standards required of show rabbits are exacting, the only way you can possibly get your rabbit up to this standard is by careful and diligent husbandry and continual training, that is training for a short spell almost everyday.

Show rabbits must be spotlessly clean

The author takes Best in Show with a young English Lop at a local agricultural show.

BRC supported shows take many different formats, they are all Star rated. A One Star show is the lowest and a Five Star the highest.

One Star Specialist Show – usually for one particular breed often with a trainee judge.

One Star Open Show – open to any breed, may be a Young Stock show in support of a higher starred Adult Show.

Two Star Specialist Show – usually for a particular breed or age catagory, only judged by a qualified judge.

Two Star Open Show – open to all breeds, only judged by qualified judge. The most common show.

Three Star Specialist Club Show – only open to members of a particular Breed Club. Breed Specialist Judge.

Three Star Championship Show – a minor Championship Show but with a Senior Breed Specialist Judge.

Four Star Championship Show – Usually an Area Championship i.e. Southern Champs.

Five Star Championship Show – there are only two of these per year, The London Championship Show held at Reading on the first weekend of September each year and the Bradford Championship Show held at the Yorkshire Show Ground, Harrogate in January each year.

These shows may take place in variety of venues:

The One and Two Star Shows usually take place in village halls up and down the country most weekends of the years.

The Three Star Shows are often held at Agricultural Shows throughout the summer - these make a great day out as the rabbit exhibitors get free entry to some of the really big shows held each summer.

Most Four Star Shows are held in Sports Centres as they are Regional Championship Shows and will have quite large entries

The Five Star Shows are held over two days so Fanciers make a holiday of their trip to the show, many take caravans to the shows and stay in them for the weekend.

PART THREE

The Rabbit Breeds: Fancy, Lop, Fur and Rex

THE FANCY BREEDS

Fancy Rabbits are an odd collection of 'exhibition' rabbits. Fur rabbits are bred for their fur, Lop rabbits for their lop ears, and Rex animals for their lustrous, smooth coats. The only thing that unites the Fancy rabbits is that they have no other use than exhibition.

Many of the Fancy breeds are in fact, very old, and have survived the vagaries of time. Individual breeds come and go in popularity, depending on fashionable trends.

In the past, the wool of the Angora rabbit has been much sought after and highly prized. For many years, Belgian Hares were exported to the USA in vast numbers, often fetching phenomenal sums.

Currently it would appear that the little red-eyed white Pole is much in demand as a show winner, whilst the popularity of the newly created Lionhead is very much in the ascendancy.

It is the diversity of the Fancy rabbits that is the strength of this section, which is a truly wonderful collection of breeds that surely has something for everybody.

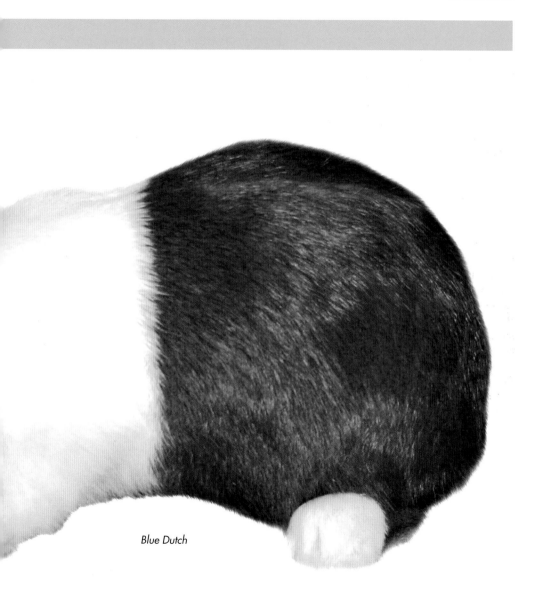

Blue Dutch

Angora

The Angora is a highly specialised rabbit that has been bred throughout history for its wool. Its long, silky hair is akin to that of the Angora goat after which it is named. It is a very ancient breed that may well have been kept by the Romans, but always for that one purpose – its wool. Whole industries have developed around the wool of the Angora rabbit, which should not be confused with that of the Angora goat. At the beginning of the nineteenth century in the Savoy area of France a whole industry sprung up hand spinning angora wool into gloves and undergarments that were light and very warm.

Two strains of Angora have been developed, the French which is a larger animal has a coat described as 'as long as possible, soft and silky and extremely dense' whilst the smaller English Angora's coat is described as 'as silky as possible, even and full all over'. The Angora is

Chinchilla Angora

unique in that its coat is multi-layered. The tips of each new coat are darker than the previous coat, which lightens, as it gains length. This produces a banding effect in the coat.

Due to the length of their coat and the special attention it requires, Angoras are not suitable as pets.

Pet Suitability	None
Good Points	For exhibition only
Poor Points	Coat requires constant care
Weight	About 7lbs (3.175kgs)
Colours	White plus a range of colours special to breed
Keep in	Hutch/Cage

Red-eyed white
English Angora

Belgian Hare

The first thing to say about the Belgian Hare is that it is not a hare. It is a rabbit that closely resembles a wild hare, and originally had very similar colouring. A true hare lives above ground rather than burrowing like a rabbit and gives birth to furred young that have their eyes open unlike the bald, blind young of the rabbit.

Although originating in the Flanders area of Belgium, it was when the Belgian Hare was brought to England in 1874 that it created a major impact on the rabbit world, firstly in Britain and later in the USA, both as an exhibition and a meat rabbit

Often described as the racehorse of the rabbit family the graceful

Belgian Hare has a long, streamlined body that arches from the shoulders to the tail. The front legs are particularly long and slender. The Hare's fur lies close to its body and is rather harsh in texture, but it is the colour of a fit Belgian Hare that is most striking. To say that it looks stunning is without doubt an understatement – maybe spectacular describes it better.

Belgian Hare Tan

Pet Suitability	★★★★
Good Points	Amenable nature
Poor Points	Quite delicate when young
Weight	8 – 9lbs (3.62 – 4.08kgs)
Colours	Rich, deep chestnut red. (Whites and Tans are now being introduced)
Keep in	Hutch/Cage

In recent years, there has been a move by a few dedicated Rabbit Fanciers to introduce a White Belgian Hare (with red eyes) and a Black and Tan coloured one. On the show bench 'type' is always more important than the colour, so if the breeders of these new colours can produce Hares in red-eyed white or black tan that have just as good a type as the traditional 'chestnut red' ones, it may not be long before we see the new colours taking top honours at the shows. Whether either of the new breeds catches on remains to be seen.

Belgian Hare

119

Dutch

The Dutch is an extremely popular rabbit that is ideal for the beginner or for any young rabbit owner. The ease with which the Dutch will settle into any situation makes it an ideal pet to live in either a hutch or in the house.

Black Dutch

Because of their compact size and robust nature they adapt readily to being handled, even by the inexperienced and thus readily endear themselves to their human companion.

Dutch does are renowned as good mothers and are often kept by fanciers to be used as foster mothers, sometimes for quite large breeds. It is not uncommon to see a little Dutch doe raising a litter of rabbits as large as English Lops in a fanciers shed.

One of the big attractions of the Dutch rabbit

Pet Suitability	★★★★★
Good Points	Temperament, Size, Hardiness
Poor Points	None
Weight	4½ lbs (2.26 kgs)
Colours	Black, Blue, Yellow, Chocolate, Tortoiseshell, Grey
Keep in	Hutch/ Cage/ Garden/ House

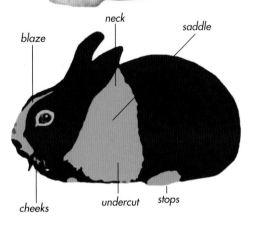

The markings of the Dutch rabbit

blaze — neck — saddle

cheeks — undercut — stops

Tort Dutch

to the fancy exhibitor is its markings, or rather, the delineation between its markings (i.e. the clean lines between the colours). The inheritance of the markings is genetic and therefore the fancier can employ skill and knowledge to try to breed the perfect specimen. Of course, there is no such thing as the perfect specimen, but many a fancier has made it their life's work to try and breed as near a perfect Dutch as possible. Some have come very close.

The markings on a Dutch rabbit have a language of their own; saddle, blaze, stops, undercut, and cheeks are the terms frequently heard when the Dutch rabbit is being judged.

Yellow Dutch

121

English

The English is the ultimate 'never say die' rabbit of the rabbit world. There is no other exhibition rabbit that so utterly defies the 'breeding for perfection' philosophy of the Fancy. Besides breeding for shape and colour, breeders must strive to achieve the markings, which affect every part of the animal from its nose to its tail. These markings not only have to be in the right position, but of a specific shape.

The consequence of the difficulties

Pet Suitability	★★★★
Good Points	Temperament, Hardiness
Poor Points	Size
Weight	6 – 8lbs (2.721 – 3.628kgs)
Colours	Black, Blue, Chocolate, Tortoiseshell, Grey
Keep in	Hutch/Cage/Garden/House

Black English with very good markings.

encountered by breeders trying to achieve the unachievable, is that many English rabbits are sold into the pet trade. But just because a rabbit has a spot or two in the wrong place, it won't be any less of a wonderful pet companion.

If the size (this is quite a big rabbit) does not deter you, then here is a wonderful, robust rabbit that should make a superb pet for either the house or garden.

Black English with poor chain and blurred spots.

The markings required of the exhibition English rabbit

HEAD MARKINGS

1. Perfect butterfly smut.
2. Circle around eyes.
3. Cheek Spots to be clear from eye circles.
4. Ears neat and clear from white.

BODY MARKINGS

1. Unbroken saddle, to be herringboned and clear in any distinct colour from base of ears to tip of tail.
2. Body or Loin Markings to be nicely broken up and not to catch the saddle.
3. Chain Markings to be as even as possible on each side.
4. Leg Markings one distinct spot on each leg.
5. Belly or Teat Spots.

Flemish Giant

As the name suggests the Flemish Giant hails from Belgium where it was originally a much larger rabbit – does in excess of 21lbs (9.525 kgs) were not uncommon. Today, exhibition does are usually between 12 and 14 lbs (5.444 – 6.35 kgs). Here is a large rabbit that will need a lot of quite careful feeding; plenty of excellent food for growth when young and then a good stable diet as an adult that keeps the rabbit in good shape and

Pet Suitability	✶✶✶✶
Good Points	Temperament, Hardiness
Poor Points	Size
Weight	Not less than 11lbs bucks – 12lbs does (4.974 – 5.44kgs)
Colours	Dark Steel Grey
Keep in	Hutch/Garden

Dark Steel Grey Flemish Giant

does not allow it to become overweight. Overweight rabbits are just as likely to fall pray to obesity-related maladies as humans are, and considerable willpower is required to regulate the adult Flemish Giant's diet.

It is not uncommon for self 'blacks' to appear in litters, however, because exhibition Flemish Giants are required to be dark steel-grey, those blacks are usually sold on by the breeders to become pets and excellent pets they can make if you have the space for such a large rabbit.

Giant Papillon

Pet Suitability	✳✳✳
Good Points	Temperament, Hardiness
Poor Points	Size
Weight	Over 11 lbs (5kgs)
Colours	Base colour is white with
	any recognised colour
	markings
Keep in	Hutch/Garden/House

This is one of the giant rabbits that may well weigh 13 to14 lbs (over 6kgs). But for its size has a fairly fine-boned skeleton, unlike the French Lop, which is of comparable size but has a heavy bone structure. The Papillon carries most of its immense weight in muscle; the front of the rabbit is very well developed with a large muscled chest and shoulders.

The most important feature of the Papillon is of course its 'butterfly' (papillon) smut nose markings. These must be well-defined, with the two 'wings' full on both sides, and only lightly touching the edges of the lower jaw.

You are unlikely to find Giant Papillion for sale in a pet shop and would have to contact a specialist breeder if you think that they could be the breed for you.

Harlequin/Magpie

If breeding English rabbits for the correct markings defines the concept of 'breeding for perfection', then breeding the Harlequin or Magpie for the show bench is surely just as demanding.

The difference between the Harlequin and the Magpie is simply colour combinations. To simplify this, let us consider the Black Harlequin, which is a combination of golden orange and dense black.

The head should be equally divided, with one half black and the other golden orange, with a clear definition

line. There should be one black ear on the orange side of the face, and an orange one on the black side. There should be one front leg orange, while the other should be black. Similarly, one hind leg should be orange ane the other black, but reversed from the

Pet Suitability	★★★★
Good Points	Temperament, Hardiness
Poor Points	Size
Weight	6 – 8 lbs (2.72 – 3.62 kgs)
Colours	See opposite
Keep in	Hutch/Garden/House

Orange and black Harlequin

Harlequin/ Magpie Colours

Black Harlequin: Dense black and golden orange.

Blue Harlequin: Lavender-blue and golden fawn.

Brown Harlequin: Rich, dark brown and golden orange.

Lilac Harlequin: Dove grey and golden fawn.

Black Magpie: Dense black and white.

Blue Magpie: Lavender-blue and white.

Brown Magpie: Rich, dark brown and white.

Lilac Magpie: Dove Grey and white.

combination at the front. As if though that were not enough, the body should be banded in black and orange, and the bands should be clearly defined.

From the description of the markings required for a show Harlequin, it is obvious that many examples of the breed will not come up to this very demanding standard. As a result, it is quite common to see them for sale in Pet Shops, and they make very fine pets indeed.

White and Black Magpie

127

Himalayan

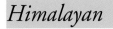

Himalayan Normal
(black points)

The Himalayan is a very old variety of rabbit believed to have originated in Asia. It is an elegant, and somewhat delicate, little rabbit whose body type is described as 'snaky'. Its coat is always white in colour, and is short and very fine. This all adds to the slight appearance of the rabbit.

Strangely, Himalayans are born all white and do not gain their coloured points until they are about three months old. It is producing a rabbit with good depth of colour in the points that is the breeders' main challenge. The coloured markings on the legs are known as 'stockings'.

Himi's are notoriously docile, passive, little

Pet Suitability	✶✶✶✶
Good Points	Temperament, Size
Poor Points	Hardiness
Weight	About 4½ lbs. (2.041 kgs)
Colours	White with points in black, blue, chocolate or lilac
Keep in	Hutch

rabbits which of course can be an advantage if you want a rabbit that will be easy to handle but a bit of a disappointment if you want a little 'character' who will entertain you.

Lionhead

The Lionhead is the new star of the rabbit world, officially recognised by the British Rabbit Council in 2002. It is fair to say that this cobby little rabbit with a mane like an African lion has taken the rabbit world, on both sides of the Atlantic, by storm.

Being the same size as the Miniature Lop, the Lionhead does not require large accommodation or a great deal of food. It is very easily kept, and is very adaptable to almost any situation. It is little wonder that the breed has become so popular.

Of course, as with any new trend, there will always be those who exploit the situation.

There are plenty of Lionheads being bred for the pet market, but be careful, check the rabbit you are buying very carefully and do not allow the heart to rule the head. Most breeders are dedicated to producing good, healthy stock but there are always some that will spoil things with irresponsible breeding.

Baby Lionheads tend to have an excess of 'furnishings' i.e. too much long hair all over

Red-eyed White Lionhead

129

Lionhead continued

Pet Suitability	✶✶✶✶✶
Good Points	Temperament, Size, Character
Poor Points	None
Weight	3 – 3½ lbs. (1.36 – 1.587 kgs.)
Colours	All BRC recognised colours
Keep in	Hutch/Cage/House/Garden

their head and bodies. As adults, they should have a mane of between two and three inches (5–8 cms) forming a full circle around the head, and falling to a fringe between the ears. They will have noticeably longer hair on the cheeks and chest, but should not have a skirt (long hair around the back end). This staged development makes it extremely difficult for the breeder or exhibitor to select the right babies to keep and those to let go. If you do wind up with a Lionhead that has long hair all around its body, it is going to require significantly more grooming than one that only has a long mane.

Young Lionhead

Adult Lionhead with a good mane

Netherland Dwarf

The Netherland Dwarf, as the name suggests, is the smallest recognised breed of rabbit. It is extremely popular with rabbit exhibitors because it requires little space, is cheap to keep, and offers the breeder an endless variety of colour and pattern to work on. However, whilst it can be trained to show itself off on the show bench, it is its temperament that has diminished its popularity as a pet. It is very easy to fall into the trap of believing this Lilliputian breed will be docile and compliant, but it may well not be. For all its diminutive size, the Netherland Dwarf can inflict a very nasty bite when it decides to do so. Of course there are many Netherland Dwarfs living happy, contented lives as pets, but it must not automatically be assumed that this will be the case. Perhaps some kind of 'take back' guarantee should be arranged with the seller at the time of purchase in case things don't work out.

Adult Marten Sable Netherland Dwarf

Netherland Dwarf cont.

Dwarf Blue Otter

REW Dwarf

Netherland Dwarf – desired 'type'

The Netherland Dwarf is short, compact, cobby and wide at the shoulders, not racy. The front legs should be short, straight, and fine in bone. Ears should be well furred, slightly rounded at the tips, not necessarily touching, and two inches in length. The head is round with a broad skull. The eyes are round, bold and bright. The fur is soft and dense.

Agouti Dwarf

Pet Suitability	✱✱✱
Good Points	Size, Cost of keeping
Poor Points	Temperament can be suspect
Weight	2 – 2½ lbs. (0.907 –1.143 kg.)
Colours	All BRC recognised colours
Keep in	Hutch/Cage

Polish

The Polish is a neat, compact, little bantam weight of a rabbit that differs from the Netherland Dwarf in that its features are quite fine, even delicate. It is a sprightly little rabbit that is known as the 'showman' of the fancy, and has probably won more top honours at shows over the years than any other breed of rabbit.

But amongst many novice exhibitors, the Pole is feared and avoided. They must be handled correctly or they will let you know in no uncertain way – with their teeth!

The coloured Poles seem to have a more placid nature than the whites, but as a whole, the breed is best left in the hands of experienced exhibitors.

Smoke Pearl Pole –
coloured Poles are usually
more placid than the whites

Polish continued

Red-eyed White Pole

Chocolate Fox Pole

Pet Suitability	None – best left in the hands of experienced exhibitors
Good Points	
Poor Points	Temperament very suspect especially in whites
Weight	2 – 2½ lbs. (0.907 – 1.143 kg)
Colours	All BRC recognised colours
Keep in	Hutch/Cage

Silver

The Silver Grey is a very old breed that was originally a 'warren rabbit' (i.e. it was kept in rabbit warrens and cropped for their valuable fur). The breed was first known as the Lincolnshire Sprig, from which it is logical to conclude that they were bred in that part of the country. They have been bred for exhibition since about 1860.

Silvers are very attractive rabbits. They are also lively and bright in disposition, making them ideal companion pets. This is a very adaptable breed that requires no special treatment.

Silvers come in four colours; black (called grey), brown (a deep rich chestnut), fawn (a deep

Pet Suitability	✳✳✳✳
Good Points	Size, Temperament, easy to keep, very adaptable
Poor Points	
Weight	5 – 6 lbs (2.267 – 2.72 kgs)
Colours	Silver Grey, Silver Fawn, Silver Brown, Silver Blue
Keep in	Hutch/Cage/House/ Garden. Show Silvers must be kept indoors to retain colour

Silver Grey

Silver continued

bright orange), and blue(a dark slate blue). The base colour is covered with silvering or ticking, which should be as even as possible over all parts of the rabbit.

For the breeder and exhibitor, the depth of the base colour and the evenness of the ticking (the silvering that covers the base colour) are important. This means that many animals that do not meet these exacting requirements find their way into the pet trade.

When the young Silvers first fur-up (at about 12 days old) they are just their base colour (black, blue, brown or fawn). They do not start to 'silver' until they are about five weeks old. If the silvering appears first at the toes, and then spreads up across the whole body there is a good chance of the all-important, even ticking. However, if the silvering appears first appears at the nose and then spreads downwards, it is highly unlikely that there will be sufficient ticking left for the toes. Unfortunately for the breeder or exhibitor, the silvering process is not likely to be completed until the youngsters are some three to four months old. It is not until this point that they can tell whether the young Silver is going to be suitable for showing, or whether it should go to the pet shop.

Fawn Silver

Tan

The Tan is a very old breed that originated from an unknown cross in a rabbit warren. The base colour (black, blue, chocolate or lilac) has rich tan-coloured markings. The eye circles, nostrils, jowls, chest, belly, flanks and underside of the tail should be a solid mass of deep, golden tan. With its fairly short, silky coat lying close to its body, a fit, young black and tan is a truly magnificent sight.

Tans that are being exhibited need to be kept in an inside rabbitry, as the effect of direct sunlight on their coats degenerates the all-important colour. But a pet Tan is a most adaptable rabbit that will readily adjust to any clean, warm, draught-free living space.

Tans are exceptionally easy rabbits to keep. They require no special food, housing or special treatment. Added to their generally amenable nature, this makes them an ideal pet.

Breeders of Tans mix the colours to improve depth and richness of shade, so it is quite likely that an exceptional Black buck will be mated to

Black tan

137

Tan continued

a Blue doe. The breeder would then hope that the richness of the blue in any Blue offspring would be improved as well as carrying the father's exceptional 'type' whilst the effect of the Blue mother on any Black youngsters in the litter would be to help increase the depth of black down the hair shaft. It is desirable for the colour to reach right down the hair shaft to the skin but sometimes the base of the hair shaft can become light (or even white). These are the kind of minor points that top breeders are working on improving in their line (successive generations of stock).

Pet Suitability	✳✳✳✳✳
Good Points	Size, Temperament, easy to keep, very adaptable
Poor Points	
Weight	4½ lbs (2.041 kgs)
Colours	Black and Tan, Blue and Tan, Chocolate and Tan, Lilac and Tan
Keep in	Hutch/Cage/House/ Garden Show Tans must be kept indoors to retain colour

Chocolate Tan

138

Thrianta

Thrianta

With its beautiful dense, soft, close coat the Thrianta 'feels' as if it should be in the Fur Section, however when the Breeds Standard Committee of the British Rabbit Council accepted the Thrianta, they placed it in with the Fancy rabbits, and there it has stayed.

The Thrianta is a firm, cobby, robust, mid-sized rabbit that is probably best kept outdoors to allow an ample dose of fresh winter air to work on the coat. A Thrianta that is kept indoors, is not likely to ever clear its coat of moult and will therefore, never achieve the wonderful lustrous rich reddish golden coat that the breed is known for.

The Thrianta is a rare breed and anyone seeking one as a pet would probably be best to contact the Rare Breeds Club at the British Rabbit Council to find a breeder who may have spare stock for sale.

Pet Suitability	✶✶✶✶✶
Good Points	Size, Temperament, easy to keep, very adaptable
Poor Points	Rare Breed – hard to find
Weight	4½ – 6 lbs. (2.041 – 2.72 kgs)
Colours	Bright intense reddish golden)
Keep in	Hutch/Garden

THE LOP BREEDS

An English Lop won at the Great Exhibition show held at Crystal Palace, London in 1851.

In recent years, the understanding of the science behind breeding and inheritance has been a driving force behind the development of new Lop breeds, but it is still worth considering where the original lop-eared rabbit came from.

How did we get from the wild rabbit weighing about 3 pounds (2.5kgs), with upright ears, that measured a mere 7½ inches (19cms) from tip to tip, and just 1⅞ inches (5cms) wide, to the English Lop that can weigh as much as 20 pounds (9kgs) and can have ears measuring up to 30 inches (76cms) long and 7½ inches (19cms) wide?

To understand the extraordinary development of Lops, we must look briefly at the domestication of the wild rabbit.

We know from ancient records that the domestication of the wild rabbit started with the Romans, who took rabbits on board their ships in cages as a ready source of fresh meat for the armies they were transporting.

After the Romans, monks perpetuated the keeping of rabbits in cages for many centuries. Using cages or rabbit courts (which are sometimes known as rabbit gardens), monks could have a ready supply of meat for all those living in the Monastery. The keeping of rabbits in enclosed spaces had two major effects on their senses. It caused the captive rabbits to become large and lazy, as they did

Crystal Palace winning Lop 1887.

not have to run from their predators. But, perhaps more importantly, they also did not need to use their ears to listen out for danger. The result of this enforced captivity was that the rabbits became bigger and the muscles in their heads that had held their ears erect became unused. When these two effects (increased size and lack of ear muscles) are added to the fact that these captive rabbits were being kept in a sheltered environment, away from the chilling effects of the wind, it explains why they became increasingly larger animals, with ears that drooped in the heat.

At the beginning of the nineteenth century some enterprising individuals from the East End of London saw how these tame, captive-bred rabbits could be used to turn a profit. Selective breeding could increase their ear size, so that the animals could be exhibited for prize money, and bets wagered on the length of their ears. This programme of selective breeding, which took place over the first half of the nineteenth century, effectively created the Lop exhibition rabbit. This animal very closely resembled the English Lop rabbit that we know today.

All current breeds of lop-eared rabbit have been developed from the English Lop, which is now known as 'The King of the Fancy'.

141

The Cashmere Lop

The Cashmere Lop is a sturdy, medium-sized rabbit with a massive head and solid, strong shoulders, which is characterised by its long coat. It has a very similar, amenable nature to its cousin the Dwarf Lop.

Red-eyed White Cashmere Lop

Seal Point Cashmere Lop

The first longhaired Cashmere Lops almost certainly appeared as mutants in litters of Dwarf Lops. The British Rabbit Council recognised the breed under the name of Cashmere Lop in the mid 1980's. Of course, the rabbit does not produce cashmere wool but its fine, soft fur strongly resembles that of the Cashmere goat from which genuine cashmere wool comes.

Cashmere Lops can be kept in hutches, although if traditional wood shavings are used as bedding, this can cause considerable problems as they become entangled in the long coat. Many exhibition specimens are kept in wire-floored cages. These have the added advantage of increased ventilation when the weather is really hot, but the wire floor can cause sore hocks, in which case the Lop should be moved back to a solid wooden-floored hutch.

The Cashmere Lop is best left in the hands of the experienced breeder/exhibitor.

Grooming Cashmere and the Miniature Cashmere Lops

To keep the Cashmere Lops long coat in a matt-free condition takes considerable time and effort. Daily grooming sessions must start whilst

Sable Mini Cashmere Lop

the Lop is still an adolescent. At this time, when the coat is particularly wayward, a ten minute-a-day grooming session will not only get on top of the developing coat but also accustom the Lop to what is going to become a feature of its daily routine.

The Miniature Cashmere Lop

As the Cashmere Lop is a long-haired version of the Dwarf Lop so the charming little Miniature Cashmere Lop, weighing no more than 3lbs 8ozs (1.6kg), is the long-haired version of the Miniature Lop. The rise in popularity of the Miniature Lop throughout the 1990's caused the development of the Miniature Cashmere Lop to be somewhat prolonged, so that it was not recognised by the British Rabbit Council until 2000.

The Miniature Cashmere Lop has the same housing and grooming requirements as the standard Cashmere Lop and is best left in the hands of experienced breeders and exhibitors.

Pet Suitability	**
Good Points	Size, Temperament
Poor Points	Coat requires constant care
Weight	4 – 5.4 lbs (2.15 – 2.381 kgs)
	Mini Cashmere Lop not to exceed 3lbs 8 ozs (1.587kgs)
Colours	All BRC recognised colours
Keep in	Hutch/Cage

Red-eyed White Mini Cashmere Lop

Dwarf Lop

The Dwarf Lop must surely be the ideal rabbit; of medium size, this robust rabbit is easy to keep and demands little apart from a clean, warm, draught-free bed, its daily rations, and a lot of affection from its owner.

Although the Dwarf Lop was first exhibited in Holland during the 1950's, it did not arrive in Britain until the 1970's and it was 1981 before Dwarf Lops were winning Best in Show at Open Shows.

Also known as the Klein (little) Widder (hanging ears), the Dwarf Lop has inherited the characteristic features that we now recognise from its ancestors. It inherited its superb dense

Red-eyed White Dwarf Lop

coat from the Chinchilla, and its multitude of different colours comes from the Netherland Dwarf.

Sooty Fawn Dwarf Lop

The Dwarf Lop is perfectly happy to run free in the house or garden. They make extremely affectionate pets, and keeping them healthy and happy will be rewarded with endless hours of fun, love, and affection. They can be comical little characters as they toss their toys around and leap gleefully in the air, and showing real enjoyment in the company of their owners.

Grooming the Dwarf Lop

Throughout most of the year, a damp hand rubbed through the coat from the tail towards the head is sufficient to remove any loose hair and keep your Dwarf Lop's coat beautiful and shiny. But, during periods of moult, these rabbits need more serious attention.

During late summer, rabbits shed their summer coat (moult) and grow a thick winter coat to keep them warm in the colder months. Their hair literally falls out by the handful, and quite frankly, they look awful. You can aid this process by daily grooming with a brush and comb (while being extremely careful not to tear the rabbit's very thin skin). A rubber scrubber designed for grooming cats is very useful for removing hair from a moulting rabbit.

Pet Suitability	✶✶✶✶✶
Good Points	Size, Temperament
Poor Points	None – although as for all flat-faced lops watch teeth
Weight	4.4 – 5.4 lbs (1.93 – 2.381 kgs)
Colours	All BRC recognised colours
Keep in	Hutch/House/Shed/ Garden

The English Lop

Agouti Butterfly English Lop

The English Lop, which is characterised by its huge ears, is a very big rabbit that is probably best kept in the hands of experienced fanciers. 'The King of the Fancy', as the English Lop is known, was first exhibited in London in 1840. The breed has been through many ups and downs since then. Currently, the breed is thriving in the USA while it is quite rare in Britain.

The English Lop has a wonderful nature. If it is kept as a house rabbit, it will take on many dog-like characteristics: sleeping on the sofa, coming and going through a dog flap in the door, and following its owner around the house. Like a dog, it will also come to dote upon its owner. However, it is not particularly keen on being picked up, and can give a very big kick to anyone trying to force it to do something it does not want to do.

As a show rabbit, it is unequalled. If the English Lop is kept correctly, and prepared correctly for showing, there is no finer rabbit placed before the judge. Unfortunately, presenting an English Lop in this perfect condition is not easy, and takes a lot of hard work and dedication.

So although the English Lop is a wonderful rabbit in many ways, it should really only be kept by an experienced pet owner or exhibitor.

Judge measuring English Lop ear length

Pet Suitability	✳✳✳
Good Points	Temperament
Poor Points	A large rabbit, ears do need looking after
Weight	10 – 12 lbs
	(4.536 – 5.443 kgs)
Colours	REW, Black, Agouti, Fawn, Sooty Fawn and all in Butterfly
Keep in	Hutch/House/Shed/ Garden

Measuring the English Lop's ears

When the English Lop is exhibited, the judge measures both the length and breadth of its ears. The judge uses a rigid 'yard stick' to measure the ear length from the tip of one ear across the top of the head to the tip of the other ear. Lops must have an ear length in excess of 20 inches (50.5 cms) to be of show standard. Ears measuring 28–30 inches (71.1–76cms) by about 7 inches (17.75cms) are considered excellent. But the Lop must still have the characteristic 'mandolin' shaped body and must conform to the British Rabbit Council breed standard. It is not just about ears.

Agouti English Lop

147

The German and French Lops

Agouti French Lop

Red-eyed White German Lop

The origins of the French Lop can be traced back to an English Lop that won the Great Exhibition show held at Crystal Palace, London in 1851. This rabbit was exported to Paris, France where it was used in cross mating with Normandy and Flemish Giants. Some of the fledgling French Lops were then exported to Germany, where, because they had come from France, they became known as French Lops. Fanciers in Britain concentrated on The Lop (the English Lop as it was later to become known), and did not import French Lops into England until the 1930s. The French Lop did not become established in Britain until the 1960's.

Orange German Lop

Agouti German Lop

The French Lop is a massive, thick set, cuddly monster of a rabbit that may well weigh in excess of 15 lbs (6.804 kgms).

Their placid, laid-back nature makes them ideal pets, especially as house-rabbits. Be warned though, they do not necessarily tolerate a dog or cat that attacks them. A French Lop

may well attack a cat or dog that has taken liberties with it, and will often come out the winner.

Although the German Lop is not as big as the French Lop, it is a very solidly built, substantial rabbit. The German Lop was developed to fill the size-gap between the Dwarf Lop and the massive French Lop. It is a highly adaptable rabbit that seems to live quite happily in almost any situation, providing it is kept warm and dry, and fed and watered correctly. Although on the large side, the German Lop makes an ideal pet that will return all the love and attention that is lavished on it by its owner.

Neither the French nor German Lop takes kindly to being stuck in a hutch at the bottom of the garden and being largely ignored. Both breeds crave human contact. A Lop that has lots of love and attention will be a contented Lop, one that is ignored and deprived of human contact may show aggression.

Pet Suitability	★★★★★
Good Points	Temperament, Hardy and robust
Poor Points	large rabbits
Weight	German Lop 6½ – 8½ lbs (2.948 – 3.855 kgs)
	French Lop over 10 lbs (over 4.536kgms)
Colours	All recognised colours
Keep in	Hutch/House/Shed/Garden

The Meissner Lop

This extremely rare Lop is characterised by the silver ticking in its very dense coat. In size, it is similar to the English Lop, being quite long in the body without having the bulk of the French Lop. Developed a hundred years ago in eastern Germany, the Meissner is a hardy animal with the ideal coat for the job. Due to the density of its coat, the Meissner is best kept in the cooler parts of the country. Even there, it does best if kept outside, or it may go into a permanent state of moult.

Due to the difficulty of getting the coat into show condition in temperate Britain, the Meissner Lop has never gained the popularity in this country that it has in continental Europe. There are usually only one or two breeders in Britain at any one time, and so it is very rare for Meissners to come up for sale.

Pet Suitability	*
Good Points	Temperament, Hardy and robust
Poor Points	Very rare – unlikely to find one
Weight	7lbs 12oz – 12lbs 12ozs (3.5kgs – 5.5kgs)
Colours	Black, Blue, Brown, Yellow
Keep in	Hutch (outdoors)

Meissner Lop

The Miniature Lop

The Miniature Lop has only been with us since the mid 1990's, but this most endearing of all the breeds has taken the rabbit world by storm. It has certainly become the star of the show.

The inquisitive, and sometimes quite comical nature of the Miniature Lop can mask its mischievous antics. Like all rabbits, Miniature Lops rest through the warmest part of the day, so early mornings and evenings are their playtimes. At these times, they are extremely playful. Anything they can find will be turned into a toy to be thrown around and... chewed.

Miniature Lops love human contact; stroking, petting, cuddling and yes, even kissing. They thrive on it, and these characteristics make them ideal pets for both adults and children.

Blue Otter Mini Lop

Black, Mini Lop

Mini Lop

The Miniature Lop continued

As its name suggest, the Miniature Lop is the smallest of the Lop breeds, weighing no more than 3lbs 8ozs (1.6kgs). But a good specimen will be a chunky little rabbit, with a massive flat-faced head and broad, strong shoulders. They should be short, broad, and well muscled with little visible neck. All in all, a good Miniature Lop should be a little powerhouse.

In the early days of the breed, malocclusion (distorted teeth) was a serious problem. The chances of it occurring now have been greatly reduced by the care shown by responsible breeders. But it is still something that should be checked when buying a Miniature Lop. If you suspect the teeth

Mini Lop Agouti

Black Otter
Mini Lop

are mis-aligned, do not allow your heart to rule your head. They will not correct themselves, and the Lop will have a life of misery while you will have a life of vet bills.

The Miniature Lop's ears should be broad, thick, well furred, and rounded at the ends. They should be carried close to the cheeks giving a horseshoe-like appearance when viewed from the front. When carried correctly, the inside of the ears should not be visible when viewed from any angle.

Black Butterfly
Mini Lop

Pet Suitability	*****
Good Points	Almost everything
Poor Points	Watch teeth
Weight	Maximum 3lbs 8ozs (1.6kgs)
Colours	All BRC recognised colours
Keep in	Hutch / House rabbit

The Miniature Lop continued

Mini Lop Sooty Fawn

Seal Point Mini Lop

Orange Mini Lop

Miniature Lion Lop

Agouti, young Lion Lop

Pet Suitability	✱✱✱✱
Good Points	Almost everything
Poor Points	Watch teeth
Weight	Maximum 3lbs 8ozs (1.6kgs)
Colours	All BRC recognised colours
Keep in	Hutch / House rabbit

hairs form a skirt around its body and rump. Because it only has the long hairs around its head, it does not present the same grooming problems as the longhaired breeds such as Angora and Cashmere Lops. Because of this, it is no more difficult to keep in good condition than any other rabbit.

Lion Lop, Blue

The Miniature Lion Lop is the newest member of the Lop family. It was produced from a cross between the Lion Head and the Miniature Lop. With its ancestors being two of today's most popular rabbits, one would expect the Lion Lop to become very popular, and for the breed to have a rosy future; but that remains to be seen.

The Miniature Lion Lop has the type and build of the Miniature Lop but has a longhaired 'lion's mane'. For exhibition purposes, it is considered a fault if the long

155

THE FUR BREEDS

As the name implies, the Fur Breeds were bred for their fur. In the Western world, there is now very little use made of rabbit fur in the manufacture of garments, but it is less than a hundred years since rabbit fur was used extensively to make some of the finest, and warmest, garments worn by both men and women.

Often called the Normal Fur Breeds the coats of these rabbits are of the type that we normally associate with rabbits. They all have strong guard hairs projecting beyond the undercoat (in the wild rabbit these are the black hairs that can readily be seen interspersed among the soft body fur). The Normal Fur Breeds differ from the Rex Fur Breeds in that the latter have shortened guard hairs, which should not project beyond the body fur.

With the decline in the use of rabbit fur the two terms 'Normal Fur Breeds' and 'Rex Fur Breeds' have evolved into the 'Fur Breeds' and the 'Rex Breeds', so although you may still hear an old fancier talking about 'Normals' the term is being used less and less these days.

The Fur Breeds are much valued for the texture and density of their coats as well as for their individual beauties of colour, shadings, shape, etc. Many of the Fur Breeds came to Britain from the Continent in the decade following the end of the First World War. They were then improved and, in some cases, recreated. Some took the name of the fur-bearing animal that they replicated, such as the Chinchilla, the Sable, and the Squirrel.

Opal British Giant

156

Alaska

The Alaska is a rather thickset, dumpy rabbit that has an intense jet-black coat. The Alaska, which was often called the 'Nubian' in England, is one of the few truly black rabbits, and is one of the most beautiful. Black rabbits became extinct in Britain but were re-introduced from Belgium in 1972.

The Alaska was a dual-purpose rabbit, having excellent meat properties as well as a dense, silky, and lustrous coat. Whilst its top coat is brilliant black with long and strong guard hairs, it has a deep blue undercoat. Its belly colour is also black, but matt.

The Alaska was created from a Himalayan x Argente x Dutch cross and was itself used in the creation of the Black Rex.

Pet Suitability	★★★★
Good Points	Size, Temperament
Poor Points	Coat will lose colour in sunlight
Weight	7 – 9 lbs (3.17 – 4.08 kgs)
Colours	Black
Keep in	Hutch/Cage/House/ Garden

Alaska

Argente

The Argente Group consists of four different coloured 'silver' rabbits. The Argente Champagne is one of the oldest known rabbits, having been mentioned in the Science Encyclopaedia of 1715. It did not have a formally recognised Standard until 1912 (in France). The breed was introduced to Britain in 1920.

All the Argentes follow the same pattern. In the nest, the coat is a self-colour. From six to eight weeks, they begin to silver, and the process is completed in approximately six to seven months.

Argente Bleu

Argente Champagne
Approx 8lbs (3.62kgs)
The Argente Champagne is the largest of the Argentes; its head is broad and rather long with a round skull whilst its body is 'moderate' in length, being neither cobby, nor racy. The Champagne has a dense, silky, glossy coat that lies loose or open rather than close to the body.

The body colour is bluish-white with a dark slate-blue undercoat. The whole of the coat is evenly and moderately interspersed with longer, jet-black hairs that give the effect of old silver or pewter, when viewed from a distance.

Argente Bleu
Approx 6lbs (2.72kgs)
The Argente Bleu is a compact and fairly cobby rabbit, that has wide, well developed hindquarters. Its very dense, glossy, silky coat

Argente Champagne

lies close to the body.

The under colour is lavender blue, whilst the body colour is bluish-white, the whole evenly and moderately interspersed with longer dark blue hairs to give a distinct bluish effect when viewed from a distance.

Argente Brun

Approx 6lbs (2.72kgs)
The Brun is physically identical to the Bleu with the same compact, cobby body.

The undercoat is as deep brown as possible with the body being a brownish-white the whole evenly and moderately interspersed with longer dark brown hairs to give a distinct brownish effect when viewed from a distance.

Pet Suitability	★★★★
Good Points	Size, Temperament
Poor Points	May be difficult to find stock
Weight	See below
Colours	Brun, Bleu, Crème, Champagne, Noir
Keep in	Hutch/Cage/House/ Garden

Argente Noir

Argente Noir

Approx 6lbs (2.72kgs)
The Argente Noir is compact with a fairly cobby body; it has a short neck with broad and rounded loins and wide well-developed hindquarters. Its short front legs are fine-boned. The Argente Noir has a very dense, glossy silky coat that lies close to the body. Its undercolour is deep slate blue with a greyish white body colour that is interspersed with longer black guard hairs to give an 'old silver' effect when viewed from a distance.

Young Argente Brun – still showing self 'baby coat' on head

159

Beveren

The Beveren is a truly utilitarian rabbit, an excellent fur rabbit, a first-rate meat rabbit, and a superb showman. They also make wonderful pets. Perhaps the only quarter where they do not excel is as a house rabbit and that is only because of their intensely dense, silky, lustrous coat, which is between 1 and 1½ inches long (2.54–3.81 cms). A coat like this really does suffer in central heating, it needs to be out in the fresh air, especially in winter when it will thicken up and show its true potential.

The Beveren has a characteristic 'mandolin' shape (as does the English Lop), which gives it a long broad back with well-developed haunches. It has a bold head with a broad muzzle and long well furred ears.

White Beveren

Blue
Perhaps the most popular colour. The coat should be light lavender blue extending to the skin.

White
For the show bench they must be pure white throughout. This colour is not easy to keep in this condition if the rabbit is running around the garden but as long as you do not want to enter any shows then does it really matter if they have stained feet. The Whites have blue eyes and are therefore known in the exhibition world as BEW's, (Blue-eyed Whites).

Black
Shortly after the arrival of the Blue Beveren from the Continent, the Black arrived. But it never did become as popular as the Blue and therefore did not have the same attention from breeders to develop it. To this day, it is quite unusual to see the lustrous black coat of the Black on the show bench.

Brown
During the 1930's breeders developed the Brown Beveren, which is often described as 'medium brown' or 'nut brown'. As with all the Beverens, it is actually the evenness of the colour throughout

Pet Suitability	****
Good Points	Size, Temperament
Poor Points	
Weight	Not less than 8lbs (3.62kgs)
Colours	Blue, White, Black, Brown, Lilac
Keep in	Hutch/Cage/Garden

Blue Beveren

the whole body that is the dominant goal of breeders and exhibitors rather than the trueness of the actual colour.

Lilac

The latest member of the Beveren family, the Lilac should be an even pink shade of dove colour throughout.

161

Blanc de Bouscat

The Blanc de Bouscat is a large, long, firm, well-muscled, snow-white rabbit that was bred from crossings between the Argente Champagne, the Angora, and the Flemish Giant by Mme Dulon of Bouscat in the Gironde region of France in 1906. It was bred as a dual-purpose rabbit; it is an excellent meat rabbit and a prolific breeder. Its litters usually consist of between seven and nine youngsters. The Blanc de Bouscat has a superb snow-white coat that has no pigmentation whatsoever, but does have guards hairs sprinkled regularly all over the coat, giving it a brilliant, frosty look.

These are not popular rabbits in Britain (they are in France) and therefore you are unlikely to find one available on the pet market and would have to seek out a specialist breeder who may well have surplus stock if you did want one.

Pet Suitability	★★★★
Good Points	Size, Temperament
Poor Points	Availability
Weight	Not less than 8lbs (3.62kgs)
Colours	Blue, White, Black, Brown, Lilac
Keep in	Hutch/Cage/Garden

Blanc de Hotot

The exact mix that was used to create the Blanc de Hotot is somewhat unclear, as Baroness Bernhard, the creator, would only admit to using 'native French spotted rabbits'. The most widely accepted theory is that they were selectively bred using the Giant Papillon Francais in combination with other breeds.

Here is another snow-white rabbit that has no pigmentation in its coat, but differs from the Blanc de Bouscat because it has black eye circles. These resemble fine spectacles, which can be considered distinctive or comical depending on your point of view.

The Blanc de Hotot is a somewhat thickset, rounded, compact rabbit with firm musculature and of average size. Its dense, soft, silky fur is said to gleam like frost.

Hotots are quite rare in Britain and may be quite difficult to get hold of.

Blanc de Hotot continued

Blanc de Hotot

Pet Suitability	★★★★
Good Points	Temperament, Size
Poor Points	Availability
Weight	8 ¾ – 9 ¾ lbs (3.96 – 4.41 kgs)
Colours	Snow White except for Black eye circles
Keep in	Hutch/Cage/Garden

Blanc de Termonde

Another of the Continental (Belgium this time) snow-white fur/meat utilitarian breeds; the Blanc de Termonde is the result of crosses between Flemish Giants and the Beveren Saint Nicholas. With its dense short coat, it is known on the Continent as a top quality fur rabbit. In Britain, it remains a rare breed, and is hardly ever seen on the show bench.

Pet Suitability	★★★★
Good Points	Temperament
Poor Points	Availability
Weight	10 – 12 lbs (4.5 – 5.4kgs)
Colours	Snow White
Keep in	Hutch/Cage/Garden

British Giant

This is the largest of the British breeds, and can reach up to twenty pounds in weight. They have a large, long, roomy body that is flat on top with broad front and hindquarters. They have a broad, large, full, bold head with erect ears and a bold eye.

The British Giant has a very dense full coat, of ¾ to 1 inch (2.5–3 cms) in length. British Giants come in six different colours. Whites can have red (REW, or Red-eyed white) or blue (BEW, or Blue-eyed white) eyes.

Anyone thinking of keeping a rabbit of this size should carefully consider the substantially different costs involved. A big rabbit needs a large hutch, which obviously involves an initially higher outlay. There are also the day-to-day running costs, such as the bedding shavings and straw that will have to be renewed every week of the rabbit's life. Not only will you have to buy a lot of bedding, you will also have to dispose of a lot of fouled bedding. Do you have some way of disposing of a substantial amount of fouled animal bedding?

Some people like little rabbits, but for those who like big ones the British Giant could be just right.

Brown Grey British Giant

Pet Suitability	★★★★
Good Points	Temperament
Poor Points	Size, Food and Housing Costs
Weight	Bucks not les than 12 ½ lbs (5.670 kgs) Does not less than 13 ½ lbs (6.123 kgs) Preferably both over 15 lbs (6.804 kgs)
Colours	White, Black, Dark Steel Grey, Blue, Brown Grey, Opal
Keep in	Hutch/Cage/Garden

Opal British Giant

165

California

Pet Suitability	✱✱✱✱
Good Points	Size, Temperament
Poor Points	
Weight	About 9 lbs (4.082 kgs)
Colours	Pure White with coloured points in Black, Chocolate, Blue, Lilac
Keep in	Hutch/Cage/Garden

Chocolate Californian

As the name suggests this is a true 'Made in the USA' breed. A Mr West bred it in California. Mr West was a furrier, who realised the need for a meat-type rabbit with a good usable pelt. Originally called the 'Cochinellas', the name was soon changed to California. In the rabbit world it is affectionately known as the 'Cali'. The Californian was imported into Britain in the 1950's and made its first major show appearance at the 1961 Bradford Championship Show.

The Californian is a white rabbit with markings, which should be as dark as possible (like those of the Himalayan). The markings are, however, the only characteristics similar to the Himalayan, for the Cali is 'very plump', 'full over and around the hips' with a saddle which should be as 'meaty as possible to nape of neck and down sides over ribs and shoulders'. Having said all this, they should be 'very firm and solid, free from over-fatness'.

The coat of the Cali is very dense but it should have enough life to resume its position immediately when rubbed in any direction. It has extremely coarse guard hairs. The points can be black (blacks are known as Normal Californians), Chocolate, Blue, or Lilac.

Chinchilla

◄ Chinchilla banding

► Chinchilla

The Chinchilla has been described as the fur rabbit par excellence. In the days when furriers sought rabbit pelts to make into clothing, it was the Chinchilla's pelt that was the most highly prized. The Chinchilla rabbit was originally bred in France to imitate the Chinchilla Lanigera, the little fur-bearing animal from the Andes, but the quality of its fur has probably surpassed that of the South American mammal.

The Chinchilla (or Chin as it is more often referred to) was first imported into Britain in 1919, and very quickly gained an enormous following amongst rabbit breeders. It should be remembered that the 1920s and 30s were

times of extreme financial difficulty for many people in Britain and here was a rabbit that would not only feed the family with high protein meat, but whose pelt was much sought after and fetched very high prices. There can be little wonder that the Chin became so popular.

Nowadays few people keep rabbits for their meat, and there is no trade for their fur, yet the Chin remains a popular exhibition rabbit amongst the lovers of the Fur breeds because of the intricacy of its colouring. If you part the fur with the edge of your hand, you will see an undercolour of dark slate-blue at the base, with a clearly defined pearly-white intermediate portion edged with a narrow black line and surmounted with grey fur, brightly ticked with black hairs. The coat is exquisitely soft, fine and dense and between 1 and 1½ inches (3–4 cms) in length.

Chinchillas are quite hardy and will happily spend their lives outside. The does make excellent mothers and are good tempered. The central heating in modern houses will prevent the Chinchilla's coat ever really achieving its glorious best, so they are far better being kept outside where their coats can bloom.

Pet Suitability	★★★★
Good Points	Size, Temperament
Poor Points	Dense Coat – heavy moulter
Weight	About 7 lbs (3.170 kgs)
Colours	To resemble the real Chinchilla
Keep in	Hutch/Cage/Garden

Chinchilla Giganta

It would be easy to say that the Chinchilla Giganta is just a giant version of the Chinchilla, but this is not quite true. Certainly, it is a much larger rabbit, but the surface of the coat is a mixture of bright blue and silver tippings interspersed with longer black- tipped guard hairs. This combination gives a 'Mackerel' effect to the coat, whilst making it a considerably darker grey than the Chinchilla rabbit.

As the name suggests this is a big rabbit; anyone considering sharing their lives with one of these giants should be aware that they are not cuddly little bunnies, and can be quite strong-willed and determined. Having said that, if they suit your lifestyle and circumstances you will be greatly rewarded with much love and attention from a devoted pet.

Pet Suitability	★★★★
Good Points	Temperament
Poor Points	Size, Dense Coat – heavy moulter
Weight	About 12 lbs (5.44 kgs)
Colours	Darker grey than the Chinchilla rabbit
Keep in	Hutch/Cage/Garden

Continental Giant

If you are the kind of person who likes Great Danes or St Bernard dogs, then this could be just the rabbit for you. The Conti (as it is always called) is above all 'big'. It is a massive, solid-looking rabbit that gives an overall impression of power. The body of the Conti should be at least 25 inches (65cms) long and its ears should be approximately one quarter the length of its body. So, the Continental Giant is a very big rabbit with very big upright ears.

Pet Suitability	✶✶✶✶
Good Points	Temperament – adorable if you like big
Poor Points	Size, Food & Housing costs
Weight	Up to 20 lbs (9kgs)
Colours	Black, Dark Steel, Light Steel, Agouti, Opal Yellow
Keep in	Hutch/Cage/Garden

Agouti Continental Giant

The Continental Giant is much bigger than the British Giant, the Chinchilla Giganta. In fact, it is bigger than all the other Giants.

If you are tempted to take on a Conti as a companion, you will need a hutch that is at least six foot long by three foot high (2m x 1m). Preferably, it should be much bigger and have a huge run attached to it, so this gentle giant can exercise properly. They need to be in contact with a variety of stimulations that will keep it interested and active and prevent it becoming lazy and fat.

Deilenaar

The Deilenaar hails from Holland, and is quite a rare rabbit in Britain. It is a very handsome, short and thickset and is a well-rounded mid-sized rabbit. It was created from the Belgian Hare, the New Zealand Red, and the Chinchilla which would account for the top colour resembling that of a Hare, a warm reddish brown with strong wavy ticking.

The Deilenaar has not really caught on in Britain and you would almost certainly have to

Pet Suitability	★★★★
Good Points	Size, Temperament
Poor Points	Quite difficult to find
Weight	About 7 ½ lbs (3.2 kgs)
Colours	Warm red – brown
Keep in	Hutch/Cage/Garden

look long and hard to find one that was for sale.

Fauve de Bourgogne

Pet Suitability	★★★
Good Points	Size, Temperament
Poor Points	Extremely rare, very difficult to find
Weight	9 – 11 lbs (4-5kgs)
Colours	Yellow/Red
Keep in	Hutch/Cage/Garden

The French created, Fauve de Bourgogne only arrived in Britain in 2005, thus making it one of the newest breeds to be accepted by the British Rabbit Council's Breeds Standards Committee.

Everything about this rabbit says 'strong'; the body is stocky, massive and well rounded, the front and rear widths are equal. The neck is short and strong. The front legs are strong and of medium length. The head is strong with a broad forehead. The ears are strong, standing firm and erect. This may only be a medium-sized rabbit but it is most definitely a robust animal.

The top colour of the Fauve is said to be a uniform yellow/red, which stretches evenly over the whole body. The fur on this super rabbit is medium in length, but it does have a very dense undercoat, which means that it would not be ideal as a house rabbit as it would be unlikely to achieve its beautiful coat if kept in a centrally heated house.

The Fauve is quite a popular rabbit in France and even has two specialist breed clubs; unfortunately the breeders in Britain can probably be counted on the fingers of one hand so it may be quite difficult to get hold of stock.

171

Silver Fox

The Silver Fox was created in Britain in the 1920s, bred to imitate the wild Silver Fox. Since then, it has grown in popularity in the rabbit exhibition world to become the number one 'fur' exhibition breed. Perhaps because it is so popular, it is relatively easy to find pet stock of the Silver Fox. Naturally, the top breeders have waiting lists for their exhibition-quality stock.

In the early days of breeding the Chinchilla, it was not unusual for a black rabbit with a white belly to turn up in a litter. It was the usual practice to destroy these odd coloured youngsters to give the looked-for Chinchillas a better chance. But when one of these black youngsters was allowed to grow up, it was found to be a beautiful black rabbit resembling the Silver Fox. With its jet-black coat, white underparts, and a profuse sprinkling of longer white hairs along its flanks and chest, it was indeed an object of great splendour. It was found that when two of these 'black' rabbits were mated together, they bred true. The rest, as they say, is history.

Black Silver Fox

Pet Suitability	★★★★★
Good Points	Size, Temperament, Availability
Poor Points	Maintaining the beautiful lustrous coat for which it is renown
Weight	About 7 ½ lbs (3.2 kgs)
Colours	Black, Blue, Chocolate, Lilac
Keep in	Hutch/Cage/Garden

Blue Silver Fox

The gleaming jet-black coat with its protruding, longer white hairs contrasting so vividly with the snow-white underneath has guaranteed the Silver Fox number one position in the show world. And as it is a hardy, robust rabbit of average size, it is also a firm favourite as a pet.

The Silver Fox now comes in Black, Blue, Chocolate, and Lilac and the breed has also been 'dwarfed' (as the Netherland Dwarf), 'lopped' (as the Mini and Dwarf Lop), and even 'rexed' (as the Tan patterned Rex).

Chocolate Silver Fox

Havana

The medium-sized Havana will naturally appeal to many because it does not need the large hutch or have the increased overheads of the giant and larger rabbit breeds. This compact little rabbit was introduced to Britain, from Holland in 1908, when it was known as Ingen Fiery Eyes on account of its eyes having a distinct 'ruby-glow' when viewed in certain lights.

Although the Americans have developed a Blue Havana, the Havana comes in only one

Pet Suitability	✺✺✺✺✺
Good Points	Size, Availability
Poor Points	Temperament – can occasionally be a bit suspect
Weight	About 5 ½ – 6 ½ lbs (2.494 – 2.948 kgs)
Colours	Rich, deep chestnut red. A rich dark chocolate with a purplish sheen
Keep in	Hutch/Cage/Garden

colour in Britain, a rich dark chocolate with a purplish sheen.

Although the Havana is a popular exhibition rabbit in its own right, it is its use in crossing-in its distinctive 'chocolate' colour to other breeds that has really established its importance.

Havana

Lilac

Essex Lavender, Cambridge Lilac, or Cambridge Blue are just some of the earlier names that were used for what we now call The Lilac. Crossing the chocolate-coloured Havana with the Blue Beveren to give a rabbit that has a dove-grey fur, which is soft, exquisitely silky, and intensely dense, created the Lilac. Like the Havana, the Lilac is compact, well-fleshed, and fine boned.

The Lilac is not particularly popular today and you may well have difficulty finding stock.

Pet Suitability	✱✱✱✱
Good Points	Size, Temperament
Poor Points	Availability
Weight	About 5 ½ – 7 lbs (2.494 – 3.17 kgs)
Colours	Pinkish shade of Dove
Keep in	Hutch/Cage/Garden

Lilac

New Zealand White

Probably the rabbit with the highest worldwide population, the New Zealand White is the archetypal 'meat rabbit' and is extremely popular wherever commercial rabbit farming is practised. Contrary to its name, this is an American-bred rabbit that was kept in its thousands at the height of the American Commercial Rabbit trade. It is said that a well-fed litter of New Zealand Whites would attain a live weight of four pounds at just eight weeks old, and this was without reducing the litter size.

Fairly long in the body, it would be difficult to find a rabbit carrying more flesh on its hind-legs. Its broad back is almost as wide at the shoulders as at the hindquarters. This was a truly dual-purpose rabbit. Furriers loved its pure white pelt, which, unlike coloured pelts, could easily be dyed to any colour, even the subtlest of pastel

Pet Suitability	✵✵✵✵✵
Good Points	Availability, Temperament
Poor Points	Size
Weight	About 11 lbs (4.989 kgs)
Colours	Bright Clean and White
Keep in	Hutch/Cage/Garden

shades. Its coat is very dense, and thick to the touch, which is neither too fine and silky, or harsh and wiry.

The commercial rabbit industry in Britain has now collapsed and those New Zealand Whites that are kept are purely for exhibition or pet purposes.

New Zealand White

New Zealand Red

Pet Suitability	✶✶✶✶
Good Points	Size Temperament
Poor Points	Availability
Weight	About 8 lbs (3.62 kgs)
Colours	Bright golden red
Keep in	Hutch/Cage/Garden

New Zealand Red

Like the New Zealand White, the New Zealand Red originated in America and is the oldest of the New Zealand breeds. At only eight pounds in weight, the Red is considerably smaller than the New Zealand White, and has a markedly different coat. Its bright golden red coat (sometimes described as reddish gold with sheen) is dense and quite harsh in texture and only ¾ inch in length (2 cms). All the other fur breeds have fur that is at least one inch (3 cms) in length, which lies close to the skin and has plenty of guard hairs.

There are still a few breeders specialising in the New Zealand Red, but it is becoming difficult to find stock to buy.

Perlfee

Perlfee

The Perlfee is little known, even in its German homeland. A fairly small, cobby rabbit that is fine-boned it has an almost invisible neck. It was bred in imitation of the Siberian Squirrel.

The Perlfee's greyish-blue coat comes in three shades; light, medium, and dark. Exhibitors prefer the medium shade. The tips of the guard hairs are light grey and dark grey and it is this colouring that gives its coat a distinctive blue-grey pearled reflection.

The Perlfee is a very rare rabbit that is unlikely to come onto the pet market.

Pet Suitability	✳✳✳
Good Points	Size Temperament
Poor Points	Availability – Rare Variety
Weight	About 5 ½ – 8 lbs (2.4 – 3.7 kgs)
Colours	Greyish Blue
Keep in	Hutch/Cage/Garden

Rhinelander

The Rhinelander is a medium-sized rabbit, which, as the name suggests, originates from Germany. The Rhinelander is one of the few tri-colour breeds; it is white with black and yellow makings. As with so many of the similarly marked rabbits, it is a breeder's nightmare. The challenge of getting the spots the right size, in the right place, and of the right colour, is one that few breeders are prepared to take on. The result is that the Rhinelander is quite a rare breed, and unless you happen to have a breeder living near you, you are unlikely to see them other than at the big Championship shows.

The Rhinelander is a thickset rabbit that is quite rounded, being the same width from front to back. It is a well-proportioned, weight-to-size rabbit that has a dense and silky coat, which is not too long.

Pet Suitability	★★★★
Good Points	Size, Temperament
Poor Points	Rare and difficult to find
Weight	6 – 9.15 lbs (2.72 – 4.41 kgs)
Colours	White base black and yellow markings
Keep in	Hutch/Cage/House/Garden

The Rhinelander

179

Sable (Siamese and Marten)

There are two types of Sables, the Marten, which has a white belly and ticking along the flanks exactly the same as the Fox, and the Siamese, which has a dark belly and no ticking. Both of them can be bred together and a proportion of each type will be represented in the resulting litter.

The Sables are another breed that owes at least a part of their genetic inheritance to the Chinchilla. Beautiful brown-shaded youngsters appeared in Chinchilla litters. When these animals were bred from, they turned out to breed true, with pelts that resembled those of the wild Sable. Both the Marten and the Siamese come in three shades; light, medium and dark. It was the medium that was originally

Siamese Sable

180

Medium Marten Sable

favoured by the exhibitors, and many perfectly good light and dark youngsters were discarded, purely because they were the wrong 'shade'. But eventually classes were introduced for each of the three shades.

A medium-sized, neat, cobby rabbit with a moderate length of body, Sables make ideal pets. They live happily in average sized hutches. They have amiable, easy going natures and are very undemanding rabbits, but respond well to lots of love and attention.

Pet Suitability	★★★★
Good Points	Size Temperament
Poor Points	
Weight	About 5 – 7 lbs (2.26 – 3.17 kgs)
Colours	Rich Sepia
Keep in	Hutch/Cage/Garden

181

Sallander

B red in the Netherlands, the Sallander is the outcome of crosses between the Thuringer, the Chinchilla, and the Marten Sable. This produced a thickset, well-rounded rabbit with very dense, silky fur that should feel very soft to the touch.

The base colour of the Sallander is a light cinnamon or pearl, while the tips of the guard hairs are brownish black. This gives an over-all 'hazed' appearance that creates a veil of pale charcoal coloured fur.

The Sallander is quite an unusual rabbit, and it would be difficult to find one for sale as a pet, as there are just so few of them around.

Sallander

Pet Suitability	✱✱✱
Good Points	Size Temperament
Poor Points	Availability
Weight	5.8 – 9.6 lbs (2.5 – 4.25kgs)
Colours	Pearl with a veil or haze of pale charcoal
Keep in	Hutch/Cage/Garden

Satin

Pet Suitability	✳✳✳✳
Good Points	Size, Temperament, Availability
Poor Points	
Weight	6 – 8 lbs (2.72 – 3.62 kgs)
Colours	In all self colours
Keep in	Hutch/Cage/Garden

The satin coat was a mutation that appeared in a litter of chocolate Havanas in the United States during the 1930's. The satin factor is a recessive characteristic. Despite this, and like the rex gene, the satin gene has now been bred into a large number of breeds. We now have satin counterparts for most rabbit breeds. The original Satin rabbits were first imported into Britain in 1947. These rabbits were mostly Ivories with pink eyes.

The Satin's coat is quite unique. It has an exquisitely smooth silky satin-like texture and sheen. It is, perhaps, the lustrous sheen that separates its coat from all others. Satins are not now very common in Britain, although they have been winners at some of the major shows in the past. In Continental Europe and the United States, the 'satinizing' of coats in all breeds is well advanced.

Ivory Satin

Siberian

The Siberian is another of the medium size 'fur' rabbits with a wonderful coat. Nobody is quite sure why it was called the Siberian because it is actually a true English creation. Mr Banfield, an Essex breeder created the breed in 1930 when trying to produce a rabbit specifically for smallholders, which would deliver a high quality pelt. He certainly succeeded, because the coat is the outstanding feature of the breed. It is believed that self-coloured English and Havana animals were used to produce the original coffee-coloured brown rabbit. Later, Blacks, Blues, and Lilacs were added.

The Breed Standard for the Siberian (usually abbreviated to the 'Sib' in the rabbit world) states the coat should be 'roll back or blanket fur' and adds: 'when turned in the reverse direction the fur must give the impression of having been sheared or pulled to expose as

Brown Siberian

few guard hairs as possible'. The result is a neat rabbit of medium size with a moderate length of body, medium boned feet and legs and a very dense, glossy fur with an exquisite texture.

With the demise of the rabbit fur trade, the 'Sib', like so many of the 'Fur' rabbits, is now, unfortunately, becoming less common and may be difficult to obtain.

Pet Suitability	✳✳✳✳✳
Good Points	Size, Temperament
Poor Points	Availability
Weight	5 – 7 lbs (2.26 – 3.17kgs)
Colours	Black, Blue, Brown, Lilac
Keep in	Hutch/Cage/Garden

Young Blue Siberian

185

Smoke Pearl

Pet Suitability	✱✱✱✱✱
Good Points	Size, Temperament,
Poor Points	Availability
Weight	5 – 7 lbs. (2.26 – 3.17 kgs)
Colours	Smoke - Marten type or Siamese type
Keep in	Hutch/Cage/Garden

Smoke Pearl

Originally known as the Smoked Beige, the Smoked Pearl is often described as 'the Sable dressed in grey'. Just like the Sable, the Smoke Pearl comes in the 'Marten' type with the chest, flanks, rump, and feet well ticked with long white hairs and belly and underside white, and also in the Siamese. The overall effect of both types is the 'smoke' appearance.

The Smoke Pearl has, as you would expect for a 'fur' rabbit, a superb coat. It is soft and very dense, with an under fur that is exquisitely silky, and exceedingly full and dense.

If you can find one, a Smoke Pearl would make a super little pet that should, for the sake of its dense coat, best be kept outside.

Sussex

The Sussex comes in two varieties, the Sussex Cream and the Sussex Gold. The difference between the two is as the name suggests, in the colour. The Gold has a cream undercolour, deepening evenly to a red-gold top colour, which is lightly ticked with cream. The shadings are described as light milk chocolate and the rabbit's eyes are reddish brown. The Cream has a pale cream undercolour, deepening evenly to a rich pinkish-cream colour, which is lightly ticked with lilac and lilac shadings. The eyes of the Cream are lilac-grey.

The Sussex is a compact, cobby medium-sized rabbit with a broad chest and well-muscled shoulders; its coat is very dense and silky with strong guard hairs.

Even if you are lucky enough to find a breeder of Sussex rabbits, and there are very few of them, then you will probably have to wait some time for one to become available. But your wait will be rewarded. The Sussex is an absolutely charming rabbit that will make anyone a super companion.

Pet Suitability	✶✶✶✶
Good Points	Size, Temperament,
Poor Points	Availability – they are quite rare
Weight	7 ½ lbs (3.39 kgs)
Colours	Reddish tortoiseshell with either brown or lilac shadings
Keep in	Hutch/Cage/Garden

Sussex Cream

Swiss Fox

The Swiss Fox is very different to all the other fur rabbits in that it is 'long haired'. The fur length of the Swiss Fox should be no longer than 2¾ inches (7 cms) and no shorter

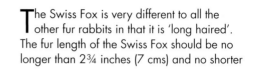

Black Swiss Fox

Pet Suitability	✱✱
Good Points	Size, Temperament,
Poor Points	Availability
Weight	5 ½ – 8 ¾ lbs (2.5 – 4 kgs)
Colours	All recognised colours
Keep in	Hutch/Cage

than 1¾ inches (4.6 cms). Although most of the fur rabbits have fur shorter than 1½ inches (4cm), there are noticeable differences in the fur length of various breeds in this category. Swiss Fox fur is slightly longer than that of the Cashmere Lop, but not quite as long as that of the Angora. The long coat is a factor that should be given careful consideration, as it will need grooming on a regular basis. For example, the Swiss Fox should not really be left to roam free in a garden where it can entangle foreign bodies in its coat.

But if you are prepared to keep the Swiss Fox as a hutch rabbit, you can have a medium to large rabbit with a strong, vigorous, well-rounded body that can make a wonderful pet.

*Blue-eyed White
Swiss Fox*

Thuringer

Thuringer

As the name suggests, the Thuringer originates from the Province of Thuringia in Germany where a schoolmaster, who crossed Himalayans, Argentes, and Giant Rabbits, created it.

The Thuringer is thickset, well-rounded rabbit with a very dense, close, short, and lustrous coat. The general colour is a yellow ochre or buff (chamois leather) colour, but the guard hairs are bluish-black in colour, which produces haze of pale charcoal. To this haze effect is added a shaded pattern in sooty (or charcoal). These sooty shadings extend over the nose, ears, chest, lower half of shoulders, flanks, rump, top of tail, legs, and belly.

The Thuringer is a very attractive rabbit that would make an ideal pet for the house or garden. However there are only a few of them about, so you could well be in for a bit of a hunt to find one.

Pet Suitability	★★★★
Good Points	Size, Temperament,
Poor Points	Availability
Weight	5.8 – 9.6 lbs.(2.5 – 4.25 kgs)
Colours	Yellow ochre with a haze of pale charcoal
Keep in	Hutch/Cage/Garden/House

Vienna Blue, Vienna White, Vienna Black

Strictly speaking, the Vienna Blue, the Vienna White, and the Vienna Black are three different breeds. Just over 100 years ago, they were quite different from one another. The White was considerably smaller than the Blue, for example. But in recent years, the three breed Standards have converged to the point where all three rabbits are described in exactly the same wording, other than for the colour.

The Vienna's are thickset, well-muscled rabbits. Whilst they are not as big as the Giants everything about them exudes strength, and they are powerful.

Pet Suitability	★★★★
Good Points	Temperament
Poor Points	Size, Availability
Weight	7.11 – 11.9 lbs (3.5 – 5.25 kgs)
Colours	Blue – dark slate-blue White – with blue eyes; Black – jet black
Keep in	Hutch/Cage/Garden

The Blues are a dark slate blue, which should be uniform over the entire body and very lustrous. Their fur is exquisitely dense, silky, and rich in guard hairs. The Whites must be a

Vienna Blue, Vienna White, Vienna Black continued

uniform pure white over the entire body, and very lustrous. The White also has that same exquisitely dense, silky coat as the Blue. Similarly, the Black must be jet black.

The Blues have always been more popular than the Whites, and the Blacks are now quite rare. The sight of a quality Vienna Blue in top show condition is a spectacle to behold. But like all the Fur rabbits, it is more about 'feel' than looks, and you really have to run your hands through the coat to appreciate the extraordinary quality of a Vienna Blue in top show condition.

The Viennas have declined in popularity in recent years in line with all of the Fur rabbits. There is no longer any market for their pelts, and they are big rabbits that needs big hutches and a lot of (expensive) food. But if you do feel that you have the time, energy, and money to keep a Vienna, they are wonderful rabbits that will return all the love and attention that you give them twice over.

Vienna White

Rare Breeds

Rare Breeds

Some of the Breeds that have now become so rare that you are unlikely to find them in Britain:

Golden Glavcot

Hulstlander

New Zealand Black

Pointed Beveren

Beige

Wheaten

Lynx (Wheaten)

Squirrel

Golden Glavcot

THE REX BREEDS

It is the coat of the Rex rabbits that distinguishes them from all other breeds of rabbit. Rex rabbits have a intensely dense, smooth, firm, plush, velvet-like coat devoid of 'guard hairs' (the coarser hairs of greater length than the body hairs that are quite normal to all breeds of rabbit).

In recent years breeders have developed a smaller version of the traditional Rex rabbit so that we now have two sizes, the Mini Rex and the Standard Rex; both come in the same varieties, although a slight anomaly arose when the Mini Rex standard was accepted in the Broken Pattern which is not an accepted pattern in the Standard Rex, the only other difference should be that the Mini Rex is about half the size of the Standard Rex.

| Mini Rex | 3½ lbs–4½ lbs (1.587–2.041 kgs) |
| Standard Rex | 6–8 lbs (2.72–3.62 kgs) |

Although Rex rabbits come in all recognised colours, it is Black and White (known as Ermine) that is by far the most popular in the exhibition world. It is quite common for the Rex to take top honours at major shows. Because of the need to keep the show specimens spotlessly clean and to prevent the sun affecting their colouring of their coats 'show' Rexes are always kept in an indoor rabbitry. However, their robust, amenable nature makes them ideal pets. So long as they have a warm, dry, draught-free hutch to sleep in, they are more

than happy to spend their lives running around the family garden, and they make excellent companion rabbits.

Unlike most other breeds of rabbit, developed by deliberately crossing two breeds that carried desired characteristics, the Rex was a genetic mutation that appeared spontaneously.

It was 1919, in the farmyard of Desire Caillon, in the Sarthe District of France that this strange 'mutation' was first seen; a rabbit minus any guard hairs. Monsieur Caillon showed this odd rabbit to the local parish priest, the Abbot Gillet. The Abbot verified that this was indeed a very different breed; and he named them Castorrex – *King of the Beavers*. He then began breeding them. However, the Abbot had no knowledge of genetics and all his stock from the farmer was so inbred that the offspring were sickly animals that did not prosper.

As in all good stories with happy endings, a wise man in the shape of the President of the French Agricultural Society, Monsieur Wiltzer, went to see the Abbot's Castorrex rabbits. It was Wiltzer who identified the 'inbreeding' problem and who recommended that the solution was to bring in an 'outcross'.

In 1925, the story continues with Professor Kohler who bought three Castorrex and crossed them with White, Black, Fawn, and Chinchilla rabbits. In 1926, he was able to show Ermine Rex, Black Rex, and Chinchilla Rex. Professor Kohler published his method in 1927. In mating Castorrex bucks to does of all the existing breeds, he was able to fix to the essential characteristics in which he was interested, colour and the absence of guard hairs.

The first Rex came to Britain in 1926 but they were extremely ugly, ungainly rabbits with oversized ears that were often called 'wrecks'. The British breeders have improved the Rex type beyond all recognition, and the heavily plushed coat we see today is a result of all their hard work.

Otter Rex

Self Rex

Black – along with the Ermine Rex the coat of the British Black Rex has been perfected by breeders to an incredibly high standard, the consequence of this is that these two colours of Rex frequently claim the highest honours at even the biggest shows in the country.

The coat of the Black Rex is a rich, lustrous blue-black, with a dark blue undercoat carried right down to the skin.

Ermine (White) – the coat of a top quality show Ermine Rex is something to behold. Half an inch (1.27 cm) in depth, the fine silky texture must be free of any harshness or wooliness. It will be intensely dense, smooth, and level over the whole body.

Needless to say, an exhibition Ermine Rex will be spotlessly clean. Yes, they really do have white feet.

Blue – perhaps because of the difficulty in maintaining the clear, bright, medium shade of blue, which should not tend to lavender, the Blue Rex has never been as popular as the

Black or Ermine. Maybe because of this difficulty in getting the colour right, it is not uncommon for those that do not quite come up to standard to be sold as pets, for which their amenable temperament is ideally suited.

Ermine Rex

Pet Suitability	★★★★★	
Good Points	Hardy, Temperament	
Poor Points	Coat will lose colour in sun	
Weight	Mini Rex	3½ lbs – 4½ lbs (1.587 – 2.041 kgs)
	Standard Rex	6 – 8 lbs (2.72 – 3.62 kgs)
Colours	Black, Ermine, Blue, Havana, Lilac, Nutria	
Keep in	Hutch/Cage/House/Garden	

Blue Rex

Havana – in the world of rabbit colours Havana is just another term for chocolate hence the Havana Rex is (or should be) a rich dark chocolate colour. If you use the edge of your hand to separate the coat, you will see that the chocolate colour goes well down the hair shaft and then there is a pearl-grey under-colour next to the skin. The Havana Rex has eyes the same colour as their coat but the eye will glow ruby-red in subdued light.

Lilac – the Lilac is not a very popular colour of Rex, its pinkish dove-grey colour is often mistaken for a poorly coloured Blue.

Nutria – even more rare than the Lilac, the Nutria Rex has a rich golden-brown coat and is extremely unusual.

Black Rex

Havana Rex

197

Shaded Rex

Smoke Pearl – the Shaded Rex are characterised by having a darker saddle from nape to tail shading off to a lighter colour on the flanks. The Smoke Pearl has a smoke-grey saddle that shades to pearl-grey on the flanks, chest, and belly. From an exhibitors point of view the shading must be gradual, avoiding blotches and streaks. The Smoke Pearl Rex also has the ruby-red glow to its eye when seen in a subdued light.

Sable Siamese – the saddle of the Sable Siamese Rex is rich sepia brown, shading gradually to a chestnut on flanks and slightly

paler on belly. Like the other Shaded Rex breeds the Sable Siamese has the ruby-red glow to its eyes when viewed in subdued lighting.

Siamese Seal Rex

Seal – the Seal has an even, rich, dark sepia head and body; the shading is only slightly paler on lower flanks, chest, and belly. The ruby-red eye is again present.

Smoke Pearl Rex

Tortoiseshell – the tortoiseshell colour in rabbits is variously known as tort, Madagascar, or sooty fawn depending on the specific breed. In Rex the colour is always called Tortoiseshell. The top colour (or saddle) is a rich orange lightly tipped with brown; the ears, muzzle, feet, belly and underside of tail are a rich blue-black that gradually shades into the body colour on the face, flanks and haunches.

Pet Suitability	★★★★★	
Good Points	Hardy, Temperament	
Poor Points	Coat will lose colour in sun	
Weight	Mini Rex	3½ lbs – 4½ lbs (1.587 – 2.041 kgs)
	Standard Rex	6 – 8 lbs (2.72 – 3.62 kgs)
Colours	Smoke Pearl, Sable Siamese, Seal, Tortoiseshell	
Keep in	Hutch/Cage/House/Garden	

Tan Pattern Rex

Tan Pattern Rex rabbits are all characterised by the distinctive markings that they have inherited from the original Black and Tan rabbit (see Fancy Breeds). Perhaps the most easily identified feature of the Tan Pattern is the 'nape triangle', which is usually white or tan depending on the breed. It appears directly behind the ears, where it is at its broadest. The triangle narrows to a point at the rear. In the actual Tan rabbit, the triangle runs into a kind of collar that encircles the neck. This is not the case in the Tan Patterned Rex breeds where it simply forms the 'nape triangle'.

Other features of the Tan Pattern are the ring of colour around each eye known as the 'eye circles'. The nostrils, jowl, chest, belly, flanks, and the under part of the tail will pick up the same colour as the eye circles, which is usually tan or white.

Marten Sable – The Martin Sables saddle is even rich sepia brown, shading gradually to a rich chestnut on flanks. The nape triangle and other markings are white.

Marten Seal – The Seal Rex, which is in the Shaded Rex, is a beautiful, rich dark sepia that only shades slightly paler to its lower flanks, chest and belly. The Marten Seal (which is a Tan Patterned Rex) has the same beautiful rich dark sepia colouring, but has a white belly, eye circles, inside of ears, underside of jowl, and nape triangle.

Fawn Rex

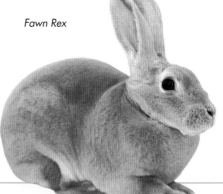

Pet Suitability	★★★★★	
Good Points	Hardy, Temperament	
Poor Points	Coat will lose colour in sun	
Weight	Mini Rex	3½ lbs – 4½ lbs (1.587 – 2.041 kgs)
	Standard Rex	6 – 8 lbs (2.72 – 3.62 kgs)
Colours	Marten Sable, Marten Seal, Orange, Fawn,Fox in Black, Blue, Chocolate, Lilac, Otter in Black, Blue, Chocolate, Lilac, Tan in Black, Blue, Chocolate, Lilac	
Keep in	Hutch/Cage/House/Garden	

Tan Rex

Fox pattern is characterised by the white ticking on the flanks and rump, which are inherited features from the Fox.

Otter (Black, Blue, Chocolate, Lilac) – The Otter pattern is characterised by the distinct border of tan colouring that divides the top colour (the Black, Blue, Chocolate or Lilac) from the creamy white of the belly, underside of chin, and tail.

Tan (Black, Blue, Chocolate, Lilac) – The Tan, Tan Pattern Rex is as near its ancestral parent in colour as possible with its belly, chest, eye circles, inside of ears, underside of jowls and nape triangle to be a beautiful rich tan colour to contrast its top colour which can be black, blue, chocolate or lilac.

Orange – The Orange Rex a truly stunning deep, rich orange colour that gradually shades to a white belly. Eye circles, inside of ears and the underside of the jowl are all white. The Orange Rex does not have a discernable nape triangle.

Otter Rex

Fawn – The Fawn rex is a bright golden fawn that has no trace of creaminess. It has a white belly, eye circles, inside of ears, underside of jowl and nape triangle.

Orange Rex

Fox (Black, Blue, Chocolate, Lilac) – The

201

Agouti Pattern Rex

Agouti is the colour of the wild rabbit, and the Agouti Pattern takes its name from the similarities with the coat pattern of the wild rabbit. If a hand is used to separate the agouti patterned rabbit's coat, so that you can see the depth of fur right down to the skin, the fur will be banded. In the Castor Rex, the fur will be a dark, rich chestnut at the top with a band of rich orange, clearly defined from the dark slate blue undercoat.

All agouti pattern rabbits have this characteristic banding, with the colours of the individual bands varying for each colour of rabbit.

Castor Rex – The Castor Rex was the original Rex rabbit (Castorrex) that the Abbot Gillet bred in France. All subsequent Rexes have been bred from the Castorrex. Whilst the Castors have lost out in the popularity stakes to the Blacks and Ermines in recent years, the sight of an in-coat Castor Rex with its rich

Lynx Rex

chestnut top coat and contrasting white belly and underside of tail is a magnificent spectacle.

Chinrex – It would be to easy to describe the Chinrex as just a 'grey' rabbit, but it is the sparkling chinchillated effect of the black and white tipped fur that characterises this magnificent rabbit. The banding on the chinchilla rex or Chinrex is dark slate blue at the base, followed by a band of white below the black and white tips.

Cinnamon – The coat of the Cinnamon Rex is a bright golden tan on the top with a band of light orange below, with a blue/grey undercoat.

Lynx – The Lynx is probably the lease common of the Agouti Patterned Rexes, and is rarely seen. But its orange coat, shot through with silver, is quite unique. The Lynx has a bright

Adult castor showing banding.

Pet Suitability	★★★★★	
Good Points	Hardy, Temperament	
Poor Points	Coat will lose colour in sun	
Weight	Mini Rex	3½ lbs – 4½ lbs (1.587 – 2.041 kgs)
	Standard Rex	6 – 8 lbs (2.72 – 3.62 kgs)
Colours	Castor, Chinrex, Cinnamon, Lynx, Opal	
Keep in	Hutch/Cage/House/Garden	

Chinchilla Rex (Chinrex)

orange band in its coat that is clearly defined from its white undercoat.

Opal – In some of the Lop breeds the blue agouti or Opal is a very popular colour. Perhaps it is because the Black, Ermine and Castor variants so dominate the Rex, that a few breeders have decided to specialise in the less common colours. The Opal Rex certainly comes into that category. The Opal's topcoat is a pale shade of blue, with a layer of golden-tan between it and the slate blue undercolour. The overall effect is of blue-shot-tan.

Rex Other Varieties

Over the years, successive generations of rabbit fanciers have sought to breed almost every pattern and colour of rabbit into the Rex. As we have seen, many have been very successful. But sometimes, despite a lifetime's work in perfecting a new colour or pattern into the Rex, the final article does not catch on with other fanciers. It is these 'Other Varieties' that come into this class.

The four main patterns in this class are not 'rare', but neither are they common. The Dalmation Rex, the Harlequin/Magpie Rex, the Himalayan Rex, and the Tri-Colour Rex are all exact copies of their parent breed, and one should refer to the notes on the originating breed for guidance on the pattern and colour.

To these four 'Other Varieties', we can add two more that are so rare that they may well not even still exist, although they are still

Astrex Ermine

recognised British Rabbit Council breeds.

The Silver Seal Rex has a jet-black coat that has an even silvering all over, giving it a sparkling effect.

Otter Mini Rex

Tri Dali

Mini Rex Broken

The Satin Rex can be in any recognised colour or pattern of Rex, but the coat has been 'satinised'. That is to say the coat has a fine satin-like texture and distinctive sheen.

The Rough Coated Rex

Even rarer than any of the previously discussed Rex Colours and Patterns are the two Rough Coated Rex, the Astrex and the Opossum. Both are so exceptionally uncommon that it is probably fairly safe to say that neither actually exists anymore, although of course there is always the chance that a genetic throwback could produce one in the future.

Himalayan Rex

Pet Suitability	★★★★★	
Good Points	Hardy, Temperament	
Poor Points	Coat will lose colour in sun	
Weight	Mini Rex	3½ lbs – 4½ lbs (1.587 – 2.041 kgs)
	Standard Rex	6 – 8 lbs (2.72 – 3.62 kgs)
Colours	Dalmation, Harlequin/Magpie, Himalayan, Tri Colour Rex	
Keep in	Hutch/Cage/House/Garden	

Index

Acknowledgements

Pat Gaskin: Fur & Feather magazine. Lisa Kelsall for use of the picture of Dylan, her Rhinelander rabbit. Emma Magnus.